without clothes, we're all naked

Carla Perez, M.D.
Author of *Getting Off The Merry-Go-Round*

Reflections on Life in the Real Lane

***Impact* 🕮 *Publishers*®**
SAN LUIS OBISPO, CALIFORNIA 93406

Library of Congress Cataloging-in-Publication Data

Perez, Carla,
    Without clothes, we're all naked : reflections on life in the real lane / Carla Perez, M.D.
            p.   cm.
    Includes bibliographical references.
    ISBN 0-915166-87-9 (trade pbk. : alk. paper)
    1. Conduct of life.   2. Perez, Carla.   I. Title.
BJ1611.P289   1995
158'.1----dc20   95-11443
                                                                       CIP

Printed in the United States of America on acid-free paper
Cover design by Sharon Schnare, San Luis Obispo, California
Cover illustration by Carl Blessing, San Francisco, California

Published by **Impact ✎ Publishers**®
POST OFFICE BOX 1094
SAN LUIS OBISPO, CALIFORNIA 93406

Contents

Preface

Acknowledgements

PROLOGUE: Your Life ---- A Three-Act Play   1

PART I. DEAL WITH THE IMPACT OF WHAT WAS
      The Past Explains Much and Excuses Little   7

1. Growing Up You Did the Best You Could   9

2. Ghosts from Childhood May Still Haunt You   19

3. Some Family Relationships Are Worth
      Salvaging...and Some Aren't   29

A SHORT INTERMISSION   44

4. It's Time to Lay the Past to Rest   49

PART II. ACCEPT THE REALITY OF WHAT IS
      Even Italians Must Stand in Line   59

5. Old Insecurities Never Die ---- They Don't Even
      Fade Away   61

6. Bad Things Happen ---- Bad Wars, Bad Bosses,
      Bad Neighbors...   72

7. Emotionally Limited Individuals
      Pop Up Everywhere   85

8. Why Don't the Villains Wear Black?   95

9. When Death Steals Loved Ones,
      It's Always Too Soon   107

ANOTHER BRIEF INTERMISSION   114

PART III. UTILIZE THE POSSIBILITY OF WHAT CAN BE
   You Can Never Have Too Many Mangos   117

10. Each Day Is a Blank Canvas   119

11. When Opportunity Knocks, Ready or Not,
    Open the Door   129

12. Choose Your Support System Carefully   139

13. A Traveling Companion Can Enhance
    Your Journey   147

14. Parenthood Brings Joy, Humility,
    and Grey Hair   158

15. Today Is All We Have ---- *Basta Cosi*   171

16. Everything Matters, Nothing Matters   175

EPILOGUE: "To Be or Not To Be"   182

FOR FURTHER READING   185

Dedication

I want to dedicate this book to many people:

My husband, Virg, who in every way has stood by me no matter what adventures and misadventures I've embarked on and stumbled into.

My children, Andrea, Michelle, Francesca, and Mario, for being who you are and keeping my priorities in focus.

Judy Abel, Leona and Scott Annis, David Cohen, Lucille Fox, Sadja Greenwood, Bob and Narai Goldsmith, Henry and Galen Hilgard, Sarah Jennings, Joe and Hama Kimura, Betty Knudson, Alan and Mary MacEwan, Alan Margolis, "Mamacita" Perez, Lynn Wagoner, and Manfred and Gloria Wolff for being true family to me over the years.

My nieces, Wendy Jacobs, Laura Barton, and especially, to Alice Jacobs ---- how wonderful to be reconnected with you.

My patients, who forever restore my faith in the fact that if you have the courage to be honest with yourself, you indeed can change.

And in memory of my brother, Frank Wolff, who never knew how much he was my hero.

I thank all of you for the roles you play or have played in my life.

Publisher's Note

This publication is designed to provide accurate and authoritative information in regard to the subject matter covered. It is sold with the understanding that the publisher is not engaged in rendering psychological, medical, or other professional services. If expert assistance or counseling is needed, the services of a competent professional should be sought.

Preface

No matter who you are ---- regardless of your age, gender, race, nationality, or economic status ---- universal challenges confront you:

- How to deal with the impact of *what was* ---- gaining perspective and being at peace with childhood and family issues;
- How to accept the reality of *what is* ---- facing each day without illusions about how life should be;
- How to utilize the possibility of *what can be* ---- making choices and building for the future as an individual, a partner, a parent.

These tasks are not easy. You may have had a less-than-ideal childhood launching, and guidelines for adult living are unclear. In addition, you may not have a supportive extended family and/or long-term relationships with friends and neighbors.

To help people meet these challenges, I began to write my version of "life as an adult" and share it with others. After my patients, friends, and relatives heard what I had to say ---- again and again and again ---- and found it helpful, I realized my pondering might help a wider audience. It was time to go public. *Without Clothes We're All Naked ---- Reflections on Life in the Real Lane* evolved out of these writings.

The ideas in the book are based on many years of professional and personal experience: twenty-four years helping patients in private psychiatric practice; fourteen years hosting a Saturday evening talk-radio show; and many years of trial-and-error ---- experience in my own life, as a wife, and as a mother of four children.

I should also mention that while writing, one night I had a vivid dream in which there were so many dirty clothes in my house, I was embarrassed to have friends visit. The next day, after a bit of soul-searching, I realized that the dream symbolized my concern about laundering too much "dirty linen" in public. Such a dilemma ---- how to stay open and honest and yet keep the trivia out.

In other words ---- this book is quite personal ---- sprinkled with vignettes about the lives of others and laced with pieces of my own saga. Some details have been changed to simplify or capture the essence of an event, and/or to protect the innocent as well as to protect me from the guilty. I have also thrown in a few magic fantasies to soften reality's rough edges.

I hope that reading the chapters will be like visiting with and hearing stories from a caring relative only a few of us are lucky enough to have ---- someone with human frailties who

- takes time out of a busy schedule to listen to you;
- encourages you not to kid yourself about whatever predicament you have gotten yourself into;

- validates your feelings and, when necessary, offers you a shoulder to cry on;
- shares personal tales of adventures and misadventures, so that you won't feel so foolish;
- and when you need it, gives you a push to move on.

Even though without clothes we're all naked, no matter who we are or what we do, if we reflect on life in the real lane together, none of us need be so alone.

Acknowledgements

Many acknowledgements are in order.

To kind friends who took time out of their busy lives to read the manuscript: Joanna Adamson, for many helpful suggestions; Duff Axom, for much encouragement; Carl Blessing, who, once he learned of the title of my book, made a most inspiring drawing of people from a number of walks of life, dressed from the front and bare from the back; John Carlson, for taking a professional photo of me, an amateur model, for the back of this book; Leigh Davidson, for giving me the idea to send the manuscript to Impact; Steve Elias for always helping no matter how many deadlines of his own he's fighting; Astra Goddard for some useful transitions; Myra Green, for catching unnecessary "psycho-babble-festing"; Douglas Johnson, for teaching me punctuation and grammar that I should have but never learned in school; Michael Krasney, who liked a juicy tidbit of my narration, but thought I best leave it out to avoid being sued; Karen Reid, for boosting my confidence; Nate Shaefler, who in his words, used to teach "anguish" and accepted me as a fellow writer; Kathe Schulz, for looking at the manuscript with a keen editor's eye; Carana Starritt, for help with suggestions for further reading; and Chris Walcoff, for cutting out some of my unnecessary verbiage.

To family members who came through with helping on yet another of "Mom's projects": Michelle, who was willing to drop whatever she was doing to add useful phrases and help smooth out draft after draft after draft; and Francesca, my youngest reader, who at sixteen filtered out several confusing words.

And to Bob Alberti, my publisher and editor, and fortunately, a psychologist, and Stephanie Hoff Strickmeier, my editor, for truly caring about the book and what it represented. They made excellent modifications; added creative gems that pulled everything together; straightened out my puzzling pronouns; and most of all, restored my faith in how wonderful it can be to work with good editors.

I greatly appreciate the help that all of you have given me.

Prologue

When you laugh, laugh like hell,
And when you get angry, get good and angry.
Try to be alive. You will be dead soon enough.
                                    ---- William Saroyan

You settle into your front-row-center seat just at curtain time, briefly glancing at the program as the house lights dim. The audience falls silent, the curtain rises. The set is vaguely familiar...the brick walk leading to the front porch, the sunny, old-fashioned living room, the vegetable garden in the sideyard...

A challenging, thought-provoking play is about to begin. One reviewer calls it "the most poignant play ever produced about the difficulty and ecstasy of one person's life!" You knew that the wait for orchestra seats was six months, but it would be worth it. Just last week the long awaited tickets finally arrived in the mail.

In the shadowy light, you try to read the program to remind yourself of the time, place, and setting of the play. Somehow the description you remember from the reviews and the set you see are surprisingly different. Maybe the dialogue among the characters will clear up your confusion.

But as the lead actor enters from stage left in the first scene, you know that this play is not the one the critics raved about.

But you're curious now. You want to see it anyway, intrigued by the subtle familiarity of the set...so much like your family's home on Elm Street. It's as if you're standing under the streetlight in front of that house instead of sitting in a semidark theater.

As the lead actor glides into the spotlight, your curiosity about the set turns to shock. It's you! You seem to be able to anticipate the actor's actions and lines just at the moment they're performed and uttered...And suddenly you are the actor and you are yourself...simultaneously.

The play is not the well-reviewed one you had planned to see. It's *Your Life!* Your opportunity has arrived ---- your chance to star in the only show in town. But there's no time to rehearse. Everyone's waiting to watch your performance. Horrors. You don't have the foggiest notion of how the script should go ---- what kind of person you should be; what you should be doing; who your costar should be, or if you should have one at all; how the plot should unfold.

You rush backstage. Frantically you scan every book you can get your hands on, eager to find one to tell you just what role you should play. No luck. Not one book describes your part. Quickly you call up your mother and father, then your friends, hoping someone will tell you what to do. Everyone you call has volumes of advice, but none of it seems right. You get a brainstorm ---- your fifth grade teacher! Her immediate reply to your telegram seems too simple: "Trust your feelings." What does that mean? Not the guidance you had hoped for. Now you're really frustrated.

Time's running out. The curtain is going up again. Should you stay in the audience and let someone else star as "you"? Do you want to settle for being the understudy? Should you go through the motions of doing your part, just reading lines written by others? The pressure mounts. You could numb yourself temporarily with alcohol, food, a quick relationship, staying busy ---- anything to not feel so nervous. What to do?

Maybe you can handle it. Maybe you can create your own script, step into center stage and develop your own role. Do you dare take the leap?

Why not? It's Act I, "Your Childhood." Break a leg!

The stage is already set by your family circumstances and the mood at this point in the action ---- happy? tragic? ---- is totally out of your control.

You hurry to get made up and put on an elegant costume, hoping the clothes will make a good impression and camouflage your insecurity. Improvising as you go, you step onto center stage and start talking, mumbling a bit to obscure the meaninglessness of your lines; you're still not at all sure what to say.

Awkward at first, the play begins to roll along fairly smoothly, though certain parts make no sense whatsoever. Instead of a simple narrative, it's full of complexities and unexpected events. Your on-stage parents are frequently busy with their own problems. They often miss their cues, rather than giving appropriate support. You try a few dance steps, hoping to catch their attention, but it doesn't work. You had counted on getting much more help from them and others.

Finally you notice a pattern in their responses and figure out the key: If you prompt everyone else on stage often enough ---- that is, if you take good enough care of them (especially your parents) ---- they perform adequately and keep you and the show going. Somehow you're able to pull it off. Everyone seems pleased; you must be doing all right. Act I of *Your Life* ends at last. The applause is reassuring.

So far so good. Feeling more comfortable, you look forward to the curtain going up on Act II, "Becoming You." Maybe this act will be less work than the last one.

You enter with self-assurance, but it doesn't last. Glancing into the front row of the audience you see your parents; their look of clear disapproval upsets you. Isn't this supposed to be *Your Life?* No one was scheduled to judge your play ---- right or wrong. You're momentarily thrown off pace, but you regain your composure and continue, realizing it's your show, not theirs.

Now more confident, you bravely move around the stage. Most of the scenes flow beautifully, though you occasionally trip over an unforeseen obstacle ---- fear, anxiety, pain, guilt, loneliness, boredom. This act is turning out to be a tough one.

Your concentration is further broken by frequent shifts of the spotlight away from you to minor characters. (Aren't they supposed to be playing supportive roles? They're competing for the lead!) With all these distracting minidramas, it's hard not to get detoured from the main plot ---- your story. But you're determined.

Somehow you have to unload the unnecessary baggage you hauled in from Act I. It's too heavy and causes a lot of needless hassle, even suffering. You then search deep within yourself to review what you learned in your crash course in acting: Focus on why you're here, what you want to be doing, and where you're going. It works! You're tempted to hold back to avoid making a fool of yourself, but you don't give in. Being tentative is a dead giveaway of your fears, so you let yourself get into the part completely, hamming it up "to the max." You're beginning to have a fantastic time!

"Becoming You" is indeed "your" act, and you're finally getting it together. Though somewhat exhausted, you enjoy hitting your stride. The audience is appreciative, and the applause for Act II even more enthusiastic.

Act III, "Meaningful Involvements," should be less lonely than the first two acts, with many more characters present. Maybe you won't have to carry the ball alone.

You're eager to strike up some close relationships. A few work out. Others don't. A short liaison with an irresponsible bit player (who can't even act) ends quickly when you realize that you're losing your identity and the action is going nowhere. You bail out in time to move on to the next scene.

It's clear that no one has properly screened the cast. Who should or shouldn't be on stage? Everyone's bickering. A few are angry; they think too much money was spent for the second act, leaving too little for this one. Others are discontented because the plot's not moving along smoothly; "Get on with your life!" is their demand. Many insist on bringing unfinished business from the first act into Act III, a dispute that never gets resolved. And there's a small group who seem to have no idea whatsoever what they're doing; they expect you to rescue them.

You feel pushed and pulled in all directions. Why doesn't the director step in and bring order? You're left completely to your own devices. Calling "time out" is impossible. Finally you escape to the wings for a moment to yourself. You let the chaos continue onstage while you think things through.

Suddenly it dawns on you! You've got to take charge. You must decide what and who enhances *Your Life* and who doesn't. Taking everything about the play into your own hands, you quickly and carefully rewrite all the dialogue, including only the cast members and action that are meaningful to you.

The task isn't easy; too often fate deals unfair blows. Players are dying, some from natural causes; others are tragically killed. Many just drift away to join other acting companies. At times losing your fellow players feels so painful, you wonder if going on is worth it. But *Your Life* is one-of-a-kind. You're determined not to give up.

Then you must face another hurdle. Intimacy. Just when it seemed you were getting your act together, you see how easily it can fall apart when you attempt the romantic scenes. Still, you're discovering that genuine closeness with another person can bring real joy.

You're ecstatic. You feel as if you have just lifted a huge weight off your shoulders; you are finally free and fully in charge of *Your Life*. At last being the star is fun. You really get into it —— dancing and singing at top speed and volume. But time is short. Already you have wasted too much of it; you don't want to regret any more lost opportunities. If only you could go back and start again, live *Your Life* forever!

As the play goes on, you've become aware that your audience has been diminishing. In fact, by the end of the third act, you are alone in the auditorium. But somehow, being alone doesn't matter; you're the director of *Your Life*. In fact, you're the playwright, performer, director, audience, and critic.

And you recognize with a flash of mature insight, *you are the only audience that your life must satisfy anyway.*

The curtain falls. You were having such a good time, you secretly hoped the whole thing was just a dress rehearsal. Not so. There are no rehearsals. This is a one-time performance.

But wait. Is it really finished? As you leave the half-light of the theater and step into the evening, you realize that *Your Life* may be over, but your life is not.

It's never too late to launch yourself.

PART I. DEAL WITH THE IMPACT OF WHAT WAS:

The Past Explains Much and Excuses Little

> *Some parts of my life should have been more carefully edited before they were released.*
> ---- Ashleigh Brilliant

Inevitably, the circumstances in which you grew up and your relationships to important family members greatly influence your adult life.

If you're lucky, your childhood provides pleasant memories, and your current relationships with significant family members are a source of mutual delight. Although your roles have evolved from child-parent to adult-adult, family get-togethers are still fun for everyone concerned. Or perhaps if there were problems in the past, they have been resolved. Maybe your father drank during your growing-up years but has recently gotten into recovery. Through a lot of discussions --- wading through his guilt and your anger and finally moving into understanding and forgiveness ---- you are able to truly enjoy your present relationship. Though you can't erase the pain of the past, your relationship with your father is no longer tainted by unresolved bad feelings.

In other cases, difficulties from the past continue into the present, and at best your current relationship is guarded; strained areas exist; conflicts remain. Perhaps your mother was always extremely critical of your appearance and friends. Though you are now married and on your own, she occasionally makes nasty remarks about your hair or outfit and offers excuses when you ask her not to criticize you. Since she has many fine qualities, and you like to get together with her and your dad, you have learned to close your ears or change the subject when she makes an unwelcome comment.

If you're unlucky, however, your growing-up years still influence your life negatively, and interactions with particular relatives may always be difficult. As a result, to this day insecurities plague you, and your parents refuse to talk about what actually happened. There might have been blatant or subtle neglect or abuse, and no one acknowledges that life was anything but perfect. This history may have thrown a dark cloud over your life, made worse by family visits.

Part I focuses on issues related to your past ---- to free you to live more fully in the present:
- getting a clearer perspective on your growing-up years;
- recognizing the ways ghosts from childhood may still haunt you;
- dealing with difficult family-of-origin relationships;
- laying your past to rest more effectively.

ONE

Growing Up You Did The Best You Could

I'm still hoping that yesterday will get better.
---- Charles Schulz's Charlie Brown

For a special family outing we had ventured to a different neighborhood Chinese restaurant, softly lit and a bit more elegant than our usual spots. Andrea, thirteen, was sharing stories about school and new friends. Michelle, four, was talking nonstop, quite full of herself, relating her day's adventure ---- feeding ducks with me. I made a throwaway comment to my husband: "Though the restaurant seems like a nice place for children, I only see grown-ups eating here." As the conversation at our table continued, I noticed that Michelle hadn't uttered a word for several minutes and in fact sat straight and looked serious.

"Are you okay?" I whispered to her. Barely moving her lips, she responded, "If I'm very quiet, will they think I'm a grown-up and let me stay?"

Children do the best they can to be accepted and avoid disapproval. With their judgement and their range of coping mechanisms, children adjust and mold themselves to be who they think their parents expect and their environments require. In healthy circumstances, no harm results from this process. Effective parents are able to give necessary support and tune into their children's needs at different stages of development without imposing unreasonable pressures and demands.

When family life is unhealthy, however, a child's desire to fit in can lead to unhappy or even disastrous consequences. Four-year-old Julia was chatting with me as I drove her home from one of my children's birthday parties: "Mommy is always mad at me. She's always mad. No matter what I do, she's mad."

I knew enough about Julia's family to recognize that her mother was a short-tempered woman who drank a lot, that her own mother, Julia's grandmother, had recently died, and that there was ongoing friction between Julia's parents. I tried to give support: "Probably your mom is upset about your grandma dying." "But I can't help it," said Julia who was starting to cry, "I can't make her all right. I can't make her happy." "What do you mean," I asked? "I can't make Grandma alive again," she answered. Julia's response was too much for me. I pulled the car over to the curb and took Julia in my arms. "It's not your fault," I told her. "You are a good girl. Your grandma died because when people get old, they eventually die. Your mom has problems because she has her own worries, and sometimes your mom and dad fight. It's not your fault, though; it's not your fault." But deep down I knew my words of reassurance would be unable to offset the misunderstandings occurring in a troubled family and their impact on a little girl too young to understand.

Three critical influences have shaped Julia's life ---- and each of ours:

- *Nature.* Genetic inheritance ---- inborn physical and personality characteristics.
- *Nurture.* Upbringing ---- the influence of parents, siblings, other people, and the environment.

* *Fate.* The luck of the draw ---- what happens in the world, often out of anyone's control ---- good and bad fortune, natural and humanmade disasters, accidents, deaths. (More about this subject in Part II.)

A few comments about nature before I continue...You were born with intellectual potential, creativity, musical, artistic, and/or athletic ability. You also had your own distinctive temperament ---- sensitivity, resilience, and a capacity to endure your own feelings and tune into those of others. From birth, you responded to your surroundings, bonding with caretakers and seeking approval (or being affected by disapproval). You had the potential to be independent and self-motivated, and you were more or less able to reach out for help.

Also, in varying degrees, you may or may not have been predisposed to depression, manic-depression, alcoholism, schizophrenia, or to particular physical illnesses such as diabetes, heart disease, cancer, arthritis, asthma, osteoporosis. You are more vulnerable to develop these conditions than someone without a genetic predisposition to them.

Parental Nurturing

Your parents, themselves the products of countless previous generations, set the stage for your life long before you entered the scene. They might have been emancipated from or still encumbered by issues from their own childhoods. Their relationship to each other might have been calm, tension-filled, or virtually nonexistent. Communication may or may not have been open and honest. Financial, medical and/or emotional difficulties might have plagued them and upstaged you. Other hardships may have occurred in the family ---- illness, divorce, death. Major social problems such as neighborhood crime, political upheaval, or war might also have existed and influenced your growing-up years. As a result of this variety of circumstances, many of which were no one's fault,

- you may have been nurtured inconsistently, in response to your parents' or other caretakers' needs more than to yours;

- your parents may not have given you a sense of emotional safety. It may have been unacceptable to show or express feelings and risky to let down your guard and be vulnerable;

- your parents may not have allowed you autonomy or encouraged you to be separate from other family members;

- your parents may have openly hurt or neglected you, or such slights could have occurred in less obvious ways;

- your parents may not have helped you learn basic social skills or how to relate to peers and move out into the world.

Jeff, a social worker recalled his experience:

My parents both worked. I was raised by whoever was the "live-in someone." They were kind but changed so often, I can't remember a single caregiver by name. I mainly remember feeling alone and scared ---- eating my way through the afternoon, playing with my dog, counting the hours and minutes until my mother came home, and then following her around everywhere. She was forever busy, into her own thoughts. I tried hard to keep my room clean and help around the house, but I could never get her sustained attention. My dad came home late, and though I know he loved me, he was gruff and not much of a communicator.

Like Jeff, you may have spent an inordinate amount of energy attempting to get minimal love, validation and support. Furthermore, if your parents were too fragile or unavailable, not only were you on your own too much, but you might have taken it upon yourself to try to support them.

When Jane was two-and-a-half, the family learned that her sister, eight years older, had leukemia; she died a year later. As a result, all through Jane's childhood, sadness pervaded the household. Her mother, a sensitive woman, became depressed and kept to herself. Her father, a shy man, took refuge in his work. Jane remembers trying endlessly to cheer her mother up, taking over the household tasks and fixing meals for her father.

One or both of your parents may have been physically and/or emotionally elsewhere ---- obsessed with work or some other activity or insulated by alcohol or another drug. Their problems may have contributed to conflicts between them, which, at minimum might have frightened you, but may have actually drawn you into their battles. In addition, your parents may have violated your emotional and/or physical boundaries, teasing or ridiculing you ---- or worse.

"How could he have done that to me!" screamed thirty-eight-year-old Marsha. "How could he. How could he." At this point she was sobbing and pounding the table. "That son of a bitch. I was only a little girl and I trusted him. He was my dad." Marsha then went on to describe an incestuous relationship her often-drunk father forced on her when she was between eleven and fifteen, a time when her mother had been ill and in and out of the hospital. Marsha continued to cry uncontrollably and couldn't speak for about fifteen minutes. "I want to kill him." In actuality, she had cut herself off from her parents while in her twenties, and her father had died shortly before she entered therapy. Marsha's story is extreme. I wish it were more uncommon.

Usually, my main sources of unhappy stories are secondhand or those my patients and I reconstruct together. Once in a while, however, I become a sad witness to an incident in someone's life as it unfolds. Though apparently minor, Chad's experience on the baseball field revealed his less-than-ideal childhood.

I had gone to watch my son Mario play in his Little League baseball game. We parents were sitting in what passed as stands ---- four rows of slightly splintered wooden benches, big enough to hold about thirty of us. Most of us didn't know each other well, but that in no way hampered us from making small talk, for we had much in common: Each of our sons was eleven or twelve years old and loved baseball and, like all parents of young athletes, we hoped our team would win on this beautiful day. The boys looked handsome in their uniforms ---- all white cotton with red hats, belts, and socks.

At one point I noticed that Chad's dad had come. For weeks Chad had looked forward to his dad seeing a game. I had only met him a few times before. A good-looking slim man, he was pleasant enough, though always rather removed, as if his mind were far away. When the game started, I focused on Mario as he took his place at second base, and I settled in, reflecting on how lucky I was to be here. Our boys were playing well.

Suddenly I was jolted out of my reverie. The opposing team was up; following a strike and a ball, the batter hit a hard line drive to Chad at third base. He caught it against his body, doubled over and fell to the ground in tears. I immediately thought that if Chad were injured, at least better it should happen when Chad's dad was here. I quickly looked over to his dad's place in the stands, expecting him to be alarmed and perhaps already on his way down to comfort Chad. Instead he glanced toward third base and continued to engage in a heated conversation with another boy's mother.

Down on the field, Chad lay on the ground, clutching his abdomen and crying. Several members of our team including my son and our coach rushed over to Chad. I again turned my head and saw Chad's dad still busy talking, unaffected by the action on the field. Holding on to one of the other boys and still crying softly, Chad got up and hobbled off to sit on the bench. The coach tried to comfort him. The game resumed when another boy was sent in to replace Chad at third base.

Chad's father continued his heated conversation. I wanted to yell at him, "Can't you see that your son is hurt? Go over and be with him!" But then I thought, if he couldn't figure this out on his own, it wasn't my business to teach him how to be a father. Fortunately Chad was not badly hurt. But something far bigger was at stake ---- a little boy's father wasn't there when he needed him, a little boy who unnecessarily cried alone.

Would Chad recall that particular day or would it blend into countless memories of a childhood filled with his dad's unavailability in times of need? Would Chad learn to numb his feelings so much that he'd lose all awareness ---- perhaps never realize ---- that these experiences even mattered? As an adult, would he always present an unruffled surface in spite of adversity? Would he become a man just like his father?

Responses To Nurturing

In Childhood. The emotional costs of a not-good-enough childhood can be high. If your parents couldn't support or protect you adequately, you had no choice but to fend for yourself using whatever means you could muster. Within your limited range of options, you could take any of a variety of paths, depending on your temperament and nature, the examples set by others around you, and the opportunities at hand.

• You may have attempted to feel okay by clinging to your parents and putting aside your own feelings and needs.

• You may have incessantly tried to be good, get high grades, not make waves ---- anything to gain approval.

• You may have stayed at a distance and physically or emotionally isolated yourself to avoid hurt and/or rejection.

• You may have become a troublemaker at home or in school to get attention.

• You may have found other relatives, neighbors, friends, teachers, or someone else to parent you.

In Adolescence. As you entered adolescence, you felt added pressures to figure out who you were and what you wanted to do in life; to fit in with peers; and to become more separate from your family.

During this time, your coping style became increasingly fixed.

• You may have tried to be popular and belong at all costs, even if it meant submerging your own personality.

• You may have looked for love in all the wrong places and possibly even become promiscuous.

• You may have used alcohol, cigarettes, or other drugs to lessen your pain.

• You may have been preoccupied with your looks, your weight, or your grades.

• You may have buried yourself in a cause, a religion, a cult, or similar group.

• You may have dropped out of school or gotten into some other kind of trouble.

If you were basically solid, these patterns afforded temporary havens to give you space and time to grow up and stand on your own feet. Unfortunately for many, however, such habits might have become permanent detours ---- self-destructive lifestyles that interfered with independence from family and the process of becoming happy, self-sustaining adults capable of being close to others.

Innate Strengths May Overcome Inadequate Nurturing

Incidentally, it's easier to understand why an individual never properly developed if we're aware of the person's history of early neglect and/or abuse, blatant or subtle. Far more puzzling is the story of someone with an unhappy family life who is able to emerge with minimum scars.

Eleanor, a college friend, grew up in a troubled family plagued by alcoholism, tension, and mixed messages. At eighteen, shortly after starting college, she married a man five years her senior and created a happy life for herself with little resemblance to her childhood.

When I ran into her several years ago, I asked what had enabled her to let go of her past and move on with her life. At first she attributed her success to her good luck in finding a supportive husband, willing to stand by while she grew up. With further thought, however, she realized that of the three children in her family, she had always been the restless one, the thoughtful one, the one who from time to time got herself into various jams, the one who didn't fit in. From early on, except for a grandfather who adored her, she couldn't turn to immediate family members for support. So she learned to rely primarily on herself.

Being by nature both curious and resourceful, she submerged herself in books and activities and fantasies of a better life. And being a likable person, she was able to meet people who essentially became her surrogate family. Perhaps more elusive, my friend's intuitive wisdom compelled her to separate herself from the craziness in her family and gain some emotional distance from them. If she didn't move on, she would drown. She was right.

When I inquired about the rest of her family, she told me that her father's alcoholism worsened and that her mother "found religion" and gradually withdrew into her own cocoon. An older sister married rich and buried her life in shopping and a jet-set life. A younger brother was a workaholic and stayed in a childless, passionless marriage. My friend was indeed the only survivor with a viable life.

* * *

It's too bad family life can't be like professional sports; if Mom isn't tuned into your needs, you can trade her for a friend's mom, who always has time to sit and listen intently to her children and is never too tired to take a walk with you. And if Dad is an unavailable workaholic, you can trade him for Johnnie's dad, a man who loves children and will shoot hoops with you whenever you ask. And while you're at it, how about trading sister Sue for one who will take you to the movies and let you borrow her sweaters. And you can get a much neater brother than Rob, the slob, though you'll have to throw some money into the deal because he is a "has been" and no one really wants him.

No. It doesn't work that way. Growing up you get the family fate deals you. Given your inner and outer resources, you make the best of the situation.

TWO

Ghosts From Childhood
May Still Haunt You

The tragedy of life is what dies inside a man while he lives.
---- Albert Schweitzer

No doubt about it: How you were raised ---- what did and did not happen in your childhood ---- influences your adult life significantly. If you were given adequate "roots" and "wings," you've probably been able to move on in life better equipped to ride the inevitable bumps in the road. You may have faced difficulties, however, if unfinished business from the past ---- ghosts that won't go away ---- haunts your adult life.

Such ghosts can choreograph your every move, locking you into preordained scripts that you may not even be aware of:

- Obvious ghosts from the past ---- apparently frozen family dramas
- Subtle ghosts ---- a different cast but the same old show
- Disguised ghosts ---- self-destructive miniplots
- Invisible ghosts ---- insecurities and anxieties

Obvious Ghosts

Some ghosts are obvious ---- the patterns in your relationships with members of your family-of-origin never move to an adult level. You might still feel trapped by the demands and expectations of a particular parent or sibling, forces which invaded your life long ago and continue to dominate it. You may possess all the outward trappings of adulthood ---- you could be well beyond twenty-one, possibly married, and even have children of your own ---- but your life is still not your own. You obviously no longer check in with your parents every hour to get permission to play with a friend, but in other ways you might be so closely bound to them that they remain too influential. Such a connection to your parents can undermine other relationships and interfere with your day-to-day functioning in and enjoyment of life.

The need for continued ties to a parent may be primarily yours. You might feel lost if you're out of touch for more than a few days or weeks. Or you'd like to have less contact but find yourself unable to shorten a phone call or resist a request no matter how intrusive or inappropriate it is. You could be eating dinner, making love, reading a story to your son, chatting with a friend. But when your parents call, you answer, putting the rest of your life on hold.

Harold, a successful insurance agent, married and the father of two young daughters, moved from Boston to San Francisco ten years ago. He and his family visit his parents for an annual family reunion in Boston, and he calls many times in between. Harold feels tense during and after each phone call, extremely anxious for several weeks before the annual reunion, unable to relax with his wife and daughters during the visit, and is unlike himself for a number of weeks afterward. His wife describes the change in Harold bluntly: "When Harold gets around his family, I feel I have no husband. He becomes the obedient child to his overly critical dad and forever tries to encourage his mom to be stronger."

Like Harold, when you visit with your parents, you may act like the child you once were.

• You become compliant to avoid criticism or confrontation, your interactions are peppered by frequent arguments, or you act overly defensive.

• After these visits are over, you feel upset or even physically ill. Maybe you overeat, overdrink, overspend, or overindulge in some other self-destructive way. You might feel angry about this pattern but find yourself unable to alter it or get yourself out of it. Incidentally, you're not alone: This scenario is common when grown children visit with their families-of-origin for holidays.

In essence, you live your life to suit your parents more than yourself. You don't dare risk offending them no matter what the cost to you. And if your parents react negatively to something you say or do, you feel hurt and guilty for days. You then expend endless energy trying to get back into their good graces. At a conscious or unconscious level, you feel that only they know what is right for you.

Furthermore, you consider it your responsibility to make your parents' lives happy and interesting. "Entertain me" was the constant plea of Anna's mother. Anna felt so indispensable to her family that anything in her own life came second. I've heard countless tales from adult children who drop everything to run over and take care of a parent who has either given up on life or alienated all potential friends and become unnecessarily helpless. (We must not, however, lump into this group parents who have led independent lives, launched their children well, and now have legitimate needs for assistance because of health problems.)

If you have infrequent contacts with parents who live far away, your dependence on them may not be obvious. Many people who migrated from the East or Midwest to the West Coast, for example, have never resolved their relationship of dependency on their families. They've simply allowed distance to seem like a solution. But the problems remain, even for those who move as far away as Hawaii or Europe.

Subtle Ghosts

Other ghosts are more subtle — variations of original unsatisfactory family dramas that you now reconstruct in new settings. As a result, you are unable to stop old, inappropriate and possibly self-defeating ways of relating to people outside your family — dates, life partners, bosses, colleagues, friends, children. In essence these relationships are infinite variations of the same drama. Though the cast has changed, the plot has not.

These dramas play out in various ways. If your parents were emotionally or physically unavailable, you may avoid any commitment to a long-term relationship, hanging on to the illusion that you just haven't found the "perfect" person yet. But actually a childhood ghost is still directing your actions. The prospect of a long-term relationship feels risky — you could lose yourself or be abandoned.

Or perhaps unconsciously you choose an emotionally or physically unavailable or abusive partner who is like your parent — workaholic, depressed, alcoholic, or lacking integrity. Then, just as when you were a child, you center your life around this person and forfeit your own needs — a condition referred to as codependency. As suffocating and unhealthy as this relationship might be, relating to such a "damaged" partner feels familiar and secure because he or she is dependent on you. In fact, you play your roles so well together that you don't see the sickness of the relationship.

Scenarios of codependency can be played out both at home and at work.

• Your husband, Louie, is never emotionally or physically available ---- forever working, unfaithful, preoccupied, drunk, stoned. You contribute ninety percent to the relationship. To dull your frustration and anger, you yourself overindulge in some activity or substance. As unsatisfactory as the whole situation is, you stay anyway. Being alone frightens you. If Louie actually leaves, you won't get over him and in fact may find a man similar to Louie to look after.

• You wait on your children hand and foot because you fear their anger. If you leave any of their requests unanswered, you feel terribly guilty. You replay with your children your unresolved conflicts with your own parents. (Note: Interactions like these can also occur when therapists, nurses, and other caretakers become overly involved with their patients, clients, or loved ones.)

• In the office, you usually do the extra jobs, even when it means working through lunch or dinner or canceling your own plans. Rather than speak up, you swallow your feelings and stoically carry on ---- and then hit the stores, the bakery, or the bar afterwards.

Instead of moving on into new relationships that compliment your adult life, you spend your adulthood re-creating childhood with parental stand-ins. Underlying your behavior is an unsatisfied hunger for unconditional love and approval. This hunger perpetuates your dependence on the applause of others ---- yet you remain caught between the fear of closeness and the terror of being alone. Your ambivalence precludes real intimacy.

Disguised Ghosts
Ghosts often hide behind disguises. You keep yourself tied to the past, trapped in irresponsible rebellious patterns

focused on food, money, work, relationships, alcohol or other drugs. You may or may not have a partner when you fall into these self-destructive patterns. One way or another, however, you are emotionally unavailable to others; your habit remains your primary love and main security.

Manuel and Eva have been married for thirty years, have two grown children, are financially well off, and to others appear to have it all. He is vice-president of a large bank; she teaches English history at a nearby college. Not lacking money, they regularly eat out with friends, share season tickets to the symphony with another couple, and travel abroad for a month every few years.

Noticed only by a few close friends are the stale vacuum within each of them and the icy communication between them. Rather than a couple sharing life together, they are like the proverbial ships passing in the night. Manuel frequently stays late at work, has had several affairs, and when at home, prefers the company of the television set over Eva. Eva regularly plays bridge with friends, keeps a meticulously clean house, and drinks too much.

Both grew up in physically intact families where parents were caught in their own compulsive patterns. Manuel's father, a high-powered executive, worked a sixty- to eighty-hour week and smoked and drank to relax. His mother was depressed, forever busy at PTA and other community meetings, and over the years, gradually put on fifty pounds.

Eva's parents barely stayed together. She described her father, who had a stable job as an accountant, as kind but mousy. He apparently was never able to stand up to her chronically angry mother, who wanted him to advance to a more prestigious, more lucrative position. Eva remembers daily arguments between her parents about money when her mother threatened to leave and her father buried himself in the newspaper.

Manuel and Eva are indeed their parents' children ---- the compulsive beat goes on.

Variations of self-destructive miniplots are endless and range from classic addictions ---- alcohol and other drugs ---- to more obscure compulsions ---- television watching, jogging. My own struggles with troublesome patterns led me to write *Getting Off The Merry-Go-Round: You Can Live Without Compulsive Habits.*

Such patterns enable you in a forbidden way to try to get what you are unable to ask for directly ---- love, attention, comfort, security, space, an easing of your pain, a numbing of your feelings. Depending on the specific addictive activity or substance, the rest of your life may be more or less affected and compromised unless you intervene to change the behavior.

If these habits go unchecked and too many important life issues are neglected, your health may deteriorate, your relationships and work may suffer, and your joy in living may fall by the wayside.

Invisible Ghosts

In many cases, life's scars are so well-concealed, the ghosts can be almost invisible. Such ghosts can lurk under a facade of competence and be covered by a preoccupation with an unhealthy relationship, camouflaged by compulsive patterns, or held in check by a "safe" lifestyle. When a job or relationship changes or you go through a life transition, however, these invisible ghosts can appear, manifesting themselves in any of a variety of forms:

- excessive insecurity, anxiety, or worry
- feelings of being rushed and driven
- inappropriate feelings of responsibility and guilt

- outbursts of anger or bouts of sadness from small provocations
- patterns of self-sabotage
- a general lack of energy and enthusiasm about anything.

If extreme, these ghosts can drain you so much, you put your dreams in storage. Amy reflected about her depression.

> *It comes over me so gradually because I'm such a damn good "coper" and my present life is essentially okay. The telltale signs of it seem petty and inconsequential. Maybe I'm just imagining the problem, making too much out of nothing.*
>
> *I get increasingly bothered by the little things my children do — the ongoing mess. I constantly have five things on my mind and have difficulty getting absorbed in any of them. I can't read anything longer than three pages. I easily flare up at my family. It takes more and more effort to get going on projects, even those for pure relaxation. I begin to feel indispensable to my husband and the kids — as if I'm selfish to take time for me. I start worrying about getting older. I become pessimistic: What's the use? It's all meaningless; nothing matters. All I want to do is sleep, and it's harder and harder to get out of bed. I start to think that maybe just plodding along is all there is to life.*
>
> *As much as I've tried to leave my unhappy childhood behind, when life is too calm, depression creeps up and chokes me. Growing up, I used to feel this way all the time.*

Rather than being caught in temporary periods of discomfort, you may have found that depression has become a way of life, especially if you have a genetic predisposition to depression. You might look fine to others and appear to function well, but the fire inside you has gone out. Days, weeks, months, and years blend into each other. Instead of facing personal challenges, you avoid them. You are reticent to be in situations that can shatter your defenses and open up old emotional wounds. As a result, you isolate yourself in an apparently safe job, relationship, and/or lifestyle but you feel trapped.

You may recognize that other people are going nowhere, but you're unaware of the ways in which your own life is stuck. Or you might realize you're stuck but not see the connection between your present dilemma and unresolved childhood issues. The bottom line: You cling to familiar ghosts for protection against a grown-up world full of "the slings and arrows of outrageous fortune." And because of this, as Jack London put it, you "exist" rather than live.

* * *

Today I'm meeting Richard for lunch. He and I go way back. Thank goodness, in spite of my cluttered life, he never leaves me. I'm running late ---- about two hours ---- you would too if you had to deal with life as I live it. For other people a get-together with a friend may be a simple matter. You just get dressed, grab your purse, and off you go. It's not that simple for me. For starters, it takes twenty minutes to get from one side of my bedroom to the other. No, I'm not a teenager stumbling through a messy room; I'm quite grown up, actually. It's just that I need to carry a lot of important baggage from my past with me; there's no way that I'm willing to give it up.

I have garbage bags full of old parts of me; they feel familiar and safe but drag me down and keep me from taking any risks: outdated self-images, bad habits, and lots of cozy childhood fears. I'm scared to death to let them go.

I can't face all this baggage, much less throw any of it out. So here it sits waiting for "some day when I'm ready." I've lost lots of friends along the way because they felt overwhelmed by my belongings. But Richard isn't one of them. He sticks by me no matter what. I guess because he's never gotten a life of his own, so he has nothing else to do except help me with mine.

I'm almost ready, but this big suitcase is bursting at the seams. Maybe I should just leave without it. No, I can't do that. I wouldn't feel complete. It's full of my father's warnings about the dangers of the world; my mother's assertions that she alone knows what's best for me; and the ugly, annoying but familiar judgements my sister imposed on me ---- "You're the one who is never going to get anywhere in life" and "Stop trying to be different, you keep embarrassing the family."

I'll have to stand on the damn bag to shut it. I only hope I won't squash and break too many old illusions. I need them to shield me from reality. Ah, at last I can snap the catch on the suitcase. Now it's just a matter of dragging everything downstairs and hailing a cab. "Hey there, you can put some of my stuff in the back seat and on the roof. I don't mind squeezing in front with you."

* * *

Richard may wait forever. The possibilities awaiting you in life won't.

THREE

Some Family Relationships Are Worth Salvaging... And Some Aren't

Fate chooses our relatives, we choose our friends.
---- Jacques Delille (1803)

amily relationships should enhance adult life. Everyone wants them to work well. After all, the people in your family ---- tied to you by blood and history ---- tried to love, protect, and launch you. You have lived through and shared a variety of experiences ---- tears and laughter, plans and dreams. Ideally an indescribable love binds you together. This is your family-of-origin, the only one you will ever have. So much of the richness of life can be gained by maintaining ties. And if you're lucky, these relationships do evolve from child-parent to adult-adult, with a minimum of difficulty and much resultant joy.

Redeemable Relationships

In some cases, family interactions temporarily become stuck in unsatisfactory ruts because people put up emotional barriers to protect themselves from those "close" to them. It might feel safer to fight than hug. Or family members may have trouble letting go of control over each other. Or they might maintain rebellious stances against relatives rather than accept responsibility for their own lives.

Another barrier to family closeness is unrealistic expectations for each other. James, a thirty-eight-year-old patient, recalled an experience with his father on a visit home during college years before.

> In the evening I said, "Hey Dad, let's walk down to the corner and get some ice cream. I'll just finish up a little more studying first." Then I went off to read. Around nine o'clock, I came back but my dad was no longer in the living room. When I couldn't find him, I asked Mom where he was. She told me he was tired and had gone to bed. I felt numb.
>
> Next morning at breakfast, I asked, "Dad ---- where were you last night? We were going to go out and get ice cream together." He mumbled something about how he'd forgotten. My God. That's the story of my whole childhood. That's just him and it hurts so much. I don't want to see it. Here I was older and only came back from college every few months, and he couldn't even remember that I had asked to do something with him, much less initiate a plan himself. God damn him.
>
> Who the hell does he think he is? I was just dying to have him notice me ---- to spend some time with me. And here I go out on a limb and ask him to get ice cream with me, and he forgets. How could he! I'm not important enough? Damn him. I am his son. What I need is so little and he forgets. He doesn't even care enough to remember.

Listening to such a story is heartbreaking. It is a variation of many told to me over the years ---- hopeful fantasies drowned by a reality, painful to accept.

My work with James centered on helping him in the following areas:

• to accept his father as he was, not through hope- colored glasses;

• to understand that if he continued to expect his father to become more emotionally available, James would forever be hurt, disappointed and angry;

• to realize that although his father most likely would not change, James could.

He had options:

• He could do as he always had, but stop being upset about the predictable way his father reacted toward him.

• He could structure visits to avoid setting himself up with unrealistic expectations, taking into account his father's emotional limits.

Although this kind of perspective doesn't correct the basic problem, it allows a problematic relationship to continue without completely disrupting a family system. It's hard enough to change a child much less expect to change a parent or a parent's long established pattern of interaction. Avoid tossing out relatives unnecessarily just because a relationship is less than perfect.

Some people who couldn't parent their little children can relate well to their grown children. When my friend Hank was five years old, his mother went off with another man and disappeared from Hank's life. Just as suddenly she reappeared when Hank was himself an adult and married with children. Although his mother had not been there for him when he grew up, she has now become a positive influence in his adult life as well as a reasonably good grandmother.

When I asked Hank how he was able to get past his anger toward his mother, he replied, "I'd already lost out on so much time with her, I didn't want to lose any more. We talked about what had happened when I was little; in no way can I excuse what my mother had done. But mainly we enjoy each other now."

More frequently, cases involve a father who abandons his child. In her thirties, Evelyn, one of my patients, decided to look up the father she had not seen since her parents divorced when she was three years old. To her surprise, her father was not a cold and rejecting man but instead a warm, though perhaps immature, weak man. He was delighted to see her. How touching that in his wallet he still carried a faded picture of three-year-old Evelyn. Evelyn readily recognized her father's weaknesses but still visits him from time to time.

A satisfactory adult-to-adult relationship with a parent who was not physically or emotionally available during your childhood cannot make up for the past. But it's not too late. In all of these instances, if relationships are now essentially healthy, problems can be dealt with and communication revitalized through awareness, effort, and if necessary, professional help. Those concerned can learn to better accept each other's separateness and differences. Why should you needlessly miss out on the chance to have the best possible relationship in adulthood?

Semiredeemable Relationships

Unfortunately, sometimes the difficulties inherent in a particular family relationship are altogether different. To the rest of the world, perhaps even to you, your relationship seems good enough. On the surface, you can work on and improve communication, but it never becomes natural and relaxed. Instead you only feel the tragic reality of a hurtful connection and an increasing legacy of unhappy memories. This result leaves you in a terrible quandary ---- where to go with an essentially derailed relationship.

Rationally it looks simple. You're all adults now. Most likely you live under different roofs, possibly miles, cities, or even continents apart. Contact may be minimal ---- occasional letters, phone calls or only short visits. Yet if you are vulnerable, the anticipation of a visit, much less the visit itself, can seriously upset you for days, or even weeks.

Other relatives, friends, and even therapists may not understand what you go through ---- what it's like to deal with Mom, Dad or Aunt Eloise. Their comments and suggestions might seem well-meaning but only make you feel worse:

- "You should try harder."
- "You should be more understanding."
- "You shouldn't be so childish."
- "Others don't react as you do ---- you are simply being too sensitive."
- "If visits affect you in this way, perhaps you need more therapy."
- "It would be selfish and mean to sharply limit contact. After all, it's your family, and you aren't in touch that much anyway."

These statements tap right into your guilt and echo the very doubts already tormenting you. For deep inside the hope for a better relationship remains ---- if you can only try again, try a bit harder, try a little differently, not be so sensitive, be more grown up, less selfish, accommodate more. Perhaps you are just imagining all the anxiety, the dread, the anger, the confusion that pervade any contacts. Maybe you're complaining too much. You might have left letters unanswered, cut phone calls short, asked a spouse or child to run interference for you. Sometimes you may have dreaded visits so much, you made up endless excuses months ahead of time to avoid seeing particular relatives on vacations or holidays.

On your own or through therapy, you could have gained insight into the difficulties of family members ---- their histories, struggles, efforts, limits ---- and your own weaknesses. But for you, maybe nothing alters the basic nightmarish scenario that predictably unfolds. One visit, one call, or even one letter from a specific parent or other relative can trip you up and carry you right back into the past. Once more you're reduced to feeling like you did when you were a child ---- inadequate, dependent, guilty, angry ---- all the emotions you've struggled so valiantly to overcome. And as was true long ago, these feelings can again become so powerful, they overcome your "adultness" completely.

You may begin to feel overwhelmed, indecisive, unreasonably anxious, seriously depressed, and worst of all, hopelessly trapped. As dramatic as these descriptions sound, if you have experienced such a phenomenon, they may seem like gross understatements. You become like a moth around a light bulb, unable to resist being drawn in and emotionally annihilated.

After an upsetting visit you might have vowed never again to put yourself through such agony. Yet habit, guilt and some kind of nameless fear prevent you from letting go of the relationship and saying a final good-bye. You continue to go through the motions of being a family and staying in touch, "'til death do you part." The words continue but the music has long ago stopped playing.

A Bit of First Aid. The puzzle feels unsolvable. How can you be a sane, responsible adult and still so easily lose yourself by contact with, or pressure to be in contact with, a particular relative? How can you explain to others what you feel when you can't even explain it to yourself? How can you make the whole mess magically vanish and enable your family to become the happy one you always wanted?

It is painful to contemplate detaching ---- emotionally and/or physically ---- from your family-of-origin. You may neglect or gradually phase out other relationships ---- with acquaintances, friends, even spouses. All too often these relationships seem frighteningly dispensable. But drastically limiting ties to a living brother or sister, much less to a parent, feels like crossing a sacred line.

Surely you can do something to make the relationship finally work. Maybe...but maybe not. Maybe you have to accept the fact that no matter what you do, staying in touch in any meaningful way is impossible.

A particular relative's impact on you may appear to make no sense. In fact, the person might not affect others in the same way at all. But your reactions are real!

Your decision to curtail a particular family relationship could be the end point of any of a number of circumstances.

• The relationship might have always been difficult; you're burned out on trying to improve it. Miranda, thirty-three, spoke of her sister who is distant from her.

> *Though I don't see her often, even an occasional phone call or an encounter at a family gathering can reduce me to feelings of complete incompetence and leave me upset for days. With each contact, I long for closeness to her. Instead I feel criticized and angry. I have written numerous letters trying to improve the relationship ---- to lessen conflicts. Nothing has helped. I guess I'll just settle for making impersonal small talk with her at family get-togethers.*

• Through therapy or on your own, you see the toll this relationship takes on you; you're unwilling to continue paying it. Kirk, forty-two, described the uneasy relationship with his father.

For as long as I can remember, my father put me down and ran over my feelings. My contacts with him bothered me for days and sometimes weeks. Therapy has made me aware of the tremendous inner price of these interactions, including undermining my marriage and contributing to my drinking problem. After much soul-searching, I see that the rest of my life is finally going well. I refuse to remain so affected by my father's negativism. I am going to have only minimal contact with him. I thought therapy would make me strong enough to be immune to his ability to erode me, but not so.

• Your relationship may have settled into a working level, dependent on all concerned being healthy and having a necessary physical and emotional distance. But life circumstances might have changed and altered your proximity and vulnerability to each other.

• A parent's or sibling's or your marriage breaks up.

• One of you moves back into the same geographic area as the other.

• One of you has a particular health or financial problem that interferes with your independence from each other. As a result, you must become more actively involved in each other's lives.

In sum, deciding if, and how, a specific troublesome family relationship can be salvaged depends on a number of factors:

• your basic ego strength

• how toxic the relative's influence is to you

• your capacity not to "rise to the bait" (or fall for it) when old "buttons" are pushed

• the physical distance separating you

• whether your shared interests and values offset the problems.

Examining these issues, you can figure out the quantity and quality of the relationship you want to sustain with the other person and how much effort and energy you're willing to expend. Discuss the dilemma with friends, relatives and even a therapist, but eventually you must decide the parameters of the relationship.

You might decide to limit contact to specific frequencies, time periods or circumstances.

• Nora visited her parents only with her husband. They would sleep in a nearby motel and stay no more than three days.

• Rebecca left as soon as her father started to drink, having explained this to him ahead of time.

• Kevin, twenty-eight, who had moved away from home for the first time, insisted his mother call no more than once a week, and never before 8:00 A.M.

• José, in his sixties, was so upset by visits with his brother Juan, he decided to stop seeing Juan altogether. Since the two live far away from each other, José can still handle letters and occasional short phone calls.

There are a whole range of possible "partial relationships" that you can work out to fit your specific circumstances and susceptibilities. They're worth trying!

Irredeemable Relationships

Some situations may warrant severing a relationship completely:

• When no matter what you do, contact with a relative resurrects so much old pain, you find yourself irretrievably catapulted back into self-destructive behavior, a deep depression, or a psychotic decompensation (i.e., mental breakdown). In addition, no amount of therapy has been able to alter this situation.

• When the relative so dramatically lacks a conscience and a capacity for guilt and remorse, contact with him or her offends your very sense of right and wrong. For example, someone who has neglected and/or abused you feels no genuine regrets about the situation.

The manipulative and downright not-so-nice people in the world are guaranteed to be someone's relatives. Unfortunately the "someone" may be you. The bottom line: If contacts continue to demolish you emotionally, you could disengage yourself; family ties need not be a life sentence.

If you feel a particular relationship is not salvageable, you can allow it to fade on its own or choose to actively let it go ---- in person, by phone, or with a well-thought-out letter. Whichever method you use, however, don't leave anything unfinished from your side. It's important that you're not left with ragged edges or regrets. When you get beyond any lingering anger, you can perhaps have at least a few positive memories. Naomi, a forty-six-year-old lawyer, described letting go of her relationship with her mother.

In spite of how happy I am now with my husband and children, when I used to visit home, my dad, now deceased, was a lifeless nonentity. And after a visit with Lena, my mother, an empty feeling would always cut through me followed by days of depression. Just like when I was a child, she was completely involved in her own thoughts. Having a conversation with her was an exercise in futility ---- she didn't listen; she changed the subject; she discounted what I said.

Sure I can see how she was a product of her own not-so-great childhood, but that doesn't excuse her for treating us as if we were servants; she made no more than token efforts to be a mother. From age one-and-a-half on, I was dumped in all-day day care or farmed off to relatives. Since age twelve, I've been pretty much on my own. My older sister and brother were treated even worse, and my younger brother was psychologically destroyed, and in essence, never left home. Since growing up was so awful, I know I overprotect my own children and even the family pets. I just don't want any living being to hurt like I used to hurt.

What's ironic is how great Lena looks to those outside our immediate family. She pays lip service to helping the less fortunate and surrounds herself with people she uses and manipulates, people at loose ends who benefit from her seeming interest. Behind their backs, however, she belittles them as if they are lower class; her involvement with them is no more than a service to her own needs. And because our family is well-respected and quite prominent in the community, nobody wants to believe how horrible our home life was.

After much therapy and a lot of pain from aborted attempts to make things all right between Lena and me, I realized she was so narcissistic, she was incapable of being a real mother. I was tired of feeling rejected and hurt; it wasn't worth it. After my father died, a well-intentioned but weak man, I decided to let my relationship with Lena go; I did so in a letter. For a couple of months after I wrote her, I felt immensely sad. But then I felt great relief. For me, Lena is so "crazy-making," staying in touch is not a viable option.

Of course you have no control over how particular relatives react to your decision to sever the ties. They may be puzzled and/or furious and never forgive you. Nor should you expect support from other family members for what you have done. You have weighed the decision carefully, however, and given all the circumstances, you feel that dropping the relationship is necessary for your mental health. You can live with that.

If you break all contact with a close relative, especially a parent, you will need to resolve feelings related to particular issues.

• You must mourn the end of the relationship and move beyond anger, blame, guilt, and sadness. Friends and other family members may not be able to help you with this difficult transition. If you feel stuck or overwhelmed by it, seek professional help.

• Many people may not understand why you have cut yourself off from the family member. They might think there was a specific misunderstanding and constantly urge you to get back in touch. When you remain firm about your decision, they may actually ostracize you. Be definite with your statements to them: "It's just too upsetting to me to have any more contact." There is no need to explain or defend your decision.

• Even years later, thoughts of seeing this parent or other relative or hearing comments by others to "just make up and let bygones be bygones" might evoke all the same old overwhelming reactions and feelings.

• From time to time, you may unexpectedly feel like an orphan with no history. How critically this feeling will affect you depends on your inner strength and other available support systems.

• Chance experiences in life can evoke feelings related to the loss of the cut-off relative: others acting toward you in the kind, thoughtful way you wished for from the family member or learning of the death of this relative.

I had not heard from Naomi for five years when she called after her mother died, asking to see me as soon as possible.

Six weeks ago, a nephew phoned me about my mother's death. I expected no inheritance —— correct. But I also learned that Lena had hoarded away a fortune and left none to my brothers and sister, none to her grandchildren, and none to all the worthy causes she professed to support. Instead, her millions went to her alma mater, Stanford, obviously to get a plaque in her name. She died like she lived, totally self-centered.

I felt numb for a couple of days. Then I pushed the whole matter to the back of my mind and thought I was done with it.

Not so. To my horror, even though everything at home and work is great, a low-level depression crept up on me, one I hadn't experienced in a long time. It's a caught, "dread" sensation, a terrible, alone feeling, probably the way I felt when I was little when Lena could never be a real mother to me. I'd meet perfect strangers, be overcome by sadness, and barely restrain myself from blurting out details of my life.

One night when I couldn't sleep, I wandered into the living room and felt an unbelievable urge to hold my dog, and then I just started sobbing. I remember doing the same thing as a child. When I was miserable, and no one was there to comfort me, I'd hug my dog and cry. Every time I realize that Lena never loved me, I feel like I'm crashing into a stone wall. Yes, I know she didn't love me because she was incapable of loving anyone. But it still hurts so much that my own mother didn't love me. I thought I'd long ago resolved my rage and pain, but her death reopened the wounds.

To help Naomi get beyond her understandable anger at Lena, during one session I offered the following poem:

Good riddance to Lena, a phony from the start.
Born self-centered, died self-centered.
No guilt, no soul, no heart.

Naomi laughed and then burst into tears. After a few more visits she was able to grieve for the good past she'd never had and put her energy back into the happy present that she'd been able to create for herself.

In situations like Naomi's, mourning is complex. You must let go of a relationship that never was...and the unrealistic hope that it ever will be.

* * *

A particular individual might be poison to one person, and at the same time, a positive force in the life of someone else. For instance, Elmer may be manipulative, completely stifling his own children, yet he offers helpful support to other people's children or to some lone adult with no family. Sophie might constantly run around like a chicken with her head cut off, always too busy to listen to her own children, yet she has endless time to talk and play with her nieces and nephews when they visit.

I'll bet you can think of an aunt, uncle, niece, nephew, cousin, sister, brother, or in-law whom you could live without. Here's a little fantasy to consider: A "Garage Sale of Unwanted Relatives" where you and your neighbors bring relatives ---- useless, intrusive, or in some other way a royal pain to you ---- and sell them for a fair price. At a minimum, the garage sale gives you a chance to get rid of unwanted relatives; they'll no longer clutter up the house. Perhaps you'll even earn a bit of pocket cash to boot. And if you're lucky, you might be able to pick up a few dandies among someone else's discards, secondhand relatives who could fit beautifully into your life.

[A note of caution: Relatives without conscience (e.g., molesters) should not be brought to the garage sale. They are universally useless and can never be cured of their potential for harm. Instead, they should be taken directly to the dump where they can be instantly compacted into a lump of junk and, once and for all, removed from circulation.]

As far-fetched as this fantasy is, many of us actually do find wonderful surrogate family members ---- relatives outside our immediate families, parents of friends, teachers, coaches, and coworkers. Though they will never one-hundred-percent replace our less-than-good-enough family-of-origin, they certainly can enrich our lives.

* * *

This chapter is presented especially for those of you who have family relationships riddled with frustration and pain, and those close to you who may not understand what you go through. Though I can't do full justice to this complex issue, I hope it helps you think about viable options. For with or without the members of your original cast, the show must go on. It is your show, not your family's. You have a right to decide who the players in it will be and what roles you want to assign to them.

A Short Intermission

Cheer up. The pleasures of being miserable are greatly overrated.

---- Anonymous

Before getting down to the nitty-gritty ---- ways to wrap up your past ---- I'm taking a break to share an astonishing turn of events from my life.

My early years were less than perfect. My mother took care of me physically, but I mainly remember how preoccupied she was with things other than my needs. I always felt it was my fault she wasn't closer to me. My father offered little more. He worked long hours, was often depressed and easy to anger, and barely communicated with other family members. As I grew older, my parents did not change, and if anything, only became more who they had always been.

At some point I became aware of how much of my adult life I was spending, trying to fill in the gaps of the past, forever giving away bits and pieces of myself in an attempt to get more response from my parents. But I was at a standstill. There must be a better way to get what I wanted.

One afternoon a bunch of us from the office got together for lunch. The conversation centered on work but finally moved to comparing our pasts. Out of the blue, one woman spoke of a new place called The Renovation Shop. She said the proprietors were able to make astounding modifications in even the toughest parents. Her parents had been quite frightful, and the shop had done a phenomenal overhaul on them. They had been cleaned up and all their bad habits removed.

The shop had only been open for three months, but its reputation for marvelous results had spread by word of mouth. In fact, it was doing such a booming business, the owners were already talking about opening a franchise. Fantastic! I decided to give it a try.

I packed up my parents and put them in the car, hoping it wasn't too late for a miracle. If I could actually update and improve them, we could become the ideal family depicted in storybooks, and we would have a whole new lease on life.

I drove to the address, full of anticipation and eager to find out the possibilities firsthand. Located in a secure neighborhood, the building, especially the outside, looked lovely, exactly as it had been described. Calmly walking toward the main door, I was soon greeted by the owner, a warm friendly man with a physique like Santa Claus. He made me feel right at home.

"What kind of parents do you want?" he asked me. Because my parents had been so emotionally unavailable in every way, I had only thought about one thing —— making them emotionally present. I never imagined I could be more specific —— order them custom-tailored to my needs.

I looked at some sample parents on display to help me choose what I wanted. They came in various heights. Since my mother was rather short, I thought about having her stretched; being taller might make her more grown up.

The floor models of fathers came with a variety of surfaces, some more colorful than others. Because my dad had been depressed, a colorful father with bright eyes would be less likely to be so drained and preoccupied. I also decided I might order longer arms for my parents. Maybe they'd be able to hug me more often, a sign of affection sorely lacking in my childhood.

This order process was certainly a challenge. I darted around the room, taking extensive notes as I listed the exact specifications to suit my needs. Then I filled out the form, marking the precise renovations and alterations and checking the box called "getting a well-matched pair." Perhaps my parents could be matched better, they wouldn't fight so much.

I handed the order to the kind proprietor. He gently led my parents to another room of the store, came back and gave me a bright red tag marked "A-1," a fine number indeed, and told me to return after three o'clock the following day. I felt lighter already. I had been carrying my parents on my back for so long, I had forgotten how much they were burdening me.

As I walked toward the street, I noticed a booth marked "Validation," something my colleagues hadn't mentioned. I went over, assuming I was to validate my parking stub. But no ---- here I myself could be validated. Unbelievable! Just what I'd spent my whole life searching for: the validation my parents were unable to give me. As I stepped into the booth, my self-esteem rose instantly. Phenomenal. Never before had I felt so confident. Filled with optimism, I got in my car and headed for home. It seemed that nirvana was less than twenty-four hours away.

When I arrived the next day to pick up my parents, I was not prepared at all for the complete transformation that had taken place. My mom and dad were smiling and looked more relaxed than I had ever seen them. In fact, I first thought the man had mixed up the claim checks and given me the wrong set of parents! Fortunately, no mistake had been made.

My mother would have greeted me by making some derogatory remark about my outfit, and my father would have glanced at his watch, rushing us and complaining about being late. But my renovated parents were completely different from the old versions. My overhauled mother, becoming teary-eyed, told me how wonderful it was to see me. My renovated father came over and gave me a big hug. Clearly the shop had done a splendid job. The metamorphosis was beyond my wildest dreams. I was so happy I started to cry.

After what seemed like an eternity of hugs between my parents and me, I was able to collect my thoughts. And it occurred to me that if parents could be changed so radically, why stop here? Maybe I could simply age-regress all of us! We could then start our family life at the beginning of my childhood. Only this time we would do it right.

I read some surprising news in the newspaper this morning. At the bottom of the third page of the classified section in bold type was an ad offering something I never dreamt actually existed: "Happy Childhoods ---- Age Regression Guaranteed or Your Money Back." And on the opposite page next to the ads for houses and apartments for rent was a "Womb Rental" section. That I'm elated is the understatement of the century. I have an appointment for ten o'clock tomorrow.

* * *

Although miracles are but a fantasy away, let's you and I return to reality. Who your parents were, and are, and what happened in your childhood may not have been fair, but most likely your parents did the best they could. The past is water under the bridge. You no longer need to be a victim of it, though. As I said in the introduction to this section, "The past explains much and excuses little." As an adult, you can choose how you see and understand the past, how much you continue to let it affect you, and how you conduct your life now. (Stay up as late as you want and eat ice cream until you burst!) Let's go on to tackle these issues.

FOUR

It's Time To Lay The Past To Rest

There is no fixing a damaged childhood.
The best you can hope for is to make the sucker float.
---- Pat Conroy, from *Prince of Tides*

L ate one night, a man called my radio show and described his current relationship with a woman, a messy relationship lacking boundaries, respect, and even love. To help him understand why on earth he got himself into such a predicament, I sought more information about his early family life. I asked him, "What do you come from?" He answered, "Iowa." Hardly the response I had anticipated, but food for thought.

Your childhood has to be like Iowa. It's what you "come from," where you grew up, how you were raised. It had pluses and minuses and is forever part of your history. But you don't need to keep being defined by it.

In order to lay your past to rest, you must face the situation directly. This process includes serious soul-searching and draining old pockets of pain, like draining a wound by cleaning it and finally allowing it to heal from the inside out. As you make corrections in your recollections and disentangle the tangled spots, be warned, it can hurt ---- especially if your past involved neglect and/or abuse, emotional or physical. Sweat and tears may flow, but the process will be temporary. Onward.

In this chapter, we're going to examine four key steps in the healing process.

• *Gather information about your childhood from your own recollections and from memories of relatives and family friends.* Try to put all of the past into perspective in as much detail as possible from your point of view as well as from that of your parents, siblings, and other family members. Look at external events affecting the family; interactions among family members; strengths and weaknesses, the triumphs and failures of all concerned. Ponder; write; share your thoughts with others.

Visits home can be a phenomenal research opportunity. Though members of your family-of-origin might have changed, by and large the basic dynamics remain. You may be able to modify some impressions and substantiate others. An acquaintance of mine who remembered feeling like an outsider while growing up visited her family after many years' absence. Sure enough, everyone talked around her as if she didn't exist. As sad as this realization was, it helped validate her memories. Family members had always told her that she was "just being too sensitive."

A forty-three-year-old colleague spoke of an episode in his life that helped round out a picture of his father.

My wife and I were taking an evening stroll around the block and encountered a friendly neighbor whom we often had seen before but had never visited with at length. One thing led to another. San Francisco being the small town that it is, it turned out that long ago he had known my parents.

He waxed on about how important my father, a teacher, had been to him while he was growing up, how my father was always there for him. A huge lump formed in my throat; I couldn't speak. I wish he had been there for me. My dad had a tough childhood and was chronically tired. I have only a handful of memories of him —— mostly of his inability to reach out to me in any way at all. I wish I had been his student.

• *Examine how as a child you responded to your family life and the ruts it has put you in as an adult.* As mentioned in Chapter 2, ghosts from the past can take many forms. These throw you into self-destructive detours that rob you of time, energy, and choices in life. To let go of them, you must connect childhood events with appropriate feelings —— anger at what shouldn't have been, sadness for what you missed, and so on —— feelings which consciously or unconsciously you may have buried within.

I met Ann, my oldest daughter, for lunch yesterday, mused a woman executive. We do that often. She is twenty-six and lives on her own across town. While eating, we spoke of this and that —— her work, my work, mutual acquaintances and friends, vacation plans, memories of her childhood —— a hodgepodge of all the important, unimportant things of life.

Afterwards, we hugged and said good-bye, and Ann rushed to get back to work. As I walked away, my eyes filled with tears —— not tears for the lovely time I had just spent with my daughter, but tears for what I had missed with my own mother. I remember my mother always being away at work or involved in her own activities. She never had time for me. I spent countless hours alone, not close to anyone, leery of depending on a soul. I still have trouble trusting others.

It's worth the effort to try to understand the connections between your past and your present life.

• *To bring completion to your healing, you need to let go of yesterday —— the illusions and disappointments, the remorse and regrets —— and mourn for the ideal childhood you'll never have.* A past with too many shortcomings is an irretrievable loss.

Some of the *why's* of your growing up years may baffle you
for as long as you live:

- "Why didn't my parents pay more attention to me?"
- "Why didn't they understand what I was feeling?"
- "Why didn't my parents hug me more?"
- "Why didn't they let me be my own person?"
- "Why did bad things happen to me?"
- "Why didn't anyone better protect me?"

You might never find good-enough answers and just have
to accept these *why's* as sad, haunting, forever unanswered
questions. What was, what wasn't, and what never can be
are history. You have only what is and what can be.

Incidentally, you must understand but not necessarily
forgive what caused your pain. Many things that happened
may have been grossly unfair, especially if there was incest
or extreme abuse. Although most parents did the best they
could, given their personalities and the circumstances at the
time, unfortunately, some parents neither tried nor cared.
Errors of the head are forgivable. Not so, errors of the heart.

I frequently urge patients and friends experiencing
unresolved matters from childhood to write letters to parents
or other relatives ---- whether these people are alive or dead.
Note that the purpose of writing the letters is to enable you
to tap into and air feelings and thoughts which continue to
trouble you, not to seek revenge. Addressing a specific
person ---- "Dear Mom" or "Dear Dad" or whomever ----
makes the communication immediate and real. You might
write the letter in a free association "right-brain" way,
pouring out feelings as they flow, much as you would write
in a personal journal. More entries can be added at different
sittings. Use any expressions that come to mind, including
strong language if that helps.

After you feel that there is no more to write, you can decide
whether or not to mail a modified version. Let me emphasize,

however, that *whether you mail the letter or not, it's the process of writing out your feelings and thoughts that helps you mend.*

Think about your motive and what you want from the other person. Would you send the letter to hurt, to assign blame, or instill guilt? If these are your reasons, keep the letter to yourself or throw it away.

Do you perhaps hope to heal an open emotional wound? To let someone know that you've been hurt? To reconcile and establish a "new" relationship? If so, and the letter says this, maybe it's a good idea to mail it. But first consider how your relative might respond if you actually sent the letter: Will this person be able to "handle" your comments? Is he or she old and frail with a weak heart or other health problems that might be worsened by your candor? Or is your relative emotionally unstable, stubborn, or unresponsive? In other words, would the letter cause more harm than good?

In short, what do you expect to accomplish with the letter? Your honest comments might "pick the scab" off an old wound better left alone. You might rid yourself of some leftover anger, but would the other person understand what you were talking about? A constructive letter, of course, may open long-broken communication ---- even become an opportunity to reconcile a lifetime of conflict between you.

Not an easy call.

Finally, I suggest that you think through, and possibly write out, how your relative ---- in keeping with his or her personality ---- would answer the letter if you were to mail it. The reply might be a variation on this theme:

I'm so surprised. I never knew you felt that way. It was such a long time ago. I think you are making too much out of nothing. After all, we did the best we could. You just blame us for your problems.

Such a response could well push your anger or guilt buttons. It certainly would not be what you hoped for. Or, if you were lucky, maybe you'd receive a letter that acknowledged your memories, explained the past, validated your feelings, and honestly apologized for unnecessary pain they may have caused you:

> *I was disappointed, but not really surprised, to know that your childhood memories are so painful. Like most parents, we meant well, but I know we made a lot of mistakes. I'm really sorry. You can be proud that you've overcome those early years and made a good life. Maybe you and I can be friends one day?*

Don't count on getting such a constructive letter. But it's possible. People do change.

How Therapy May Help

Although you can work through these issues on your own, therapy may speed up the process. Contrary to popular belief, most people who seek professional help are among the strong ones. They're fighters, survivors, individuals who have had the courage to look squarely at their lives and declare: "Something is not right. There must be more to life, and I want it." Cloaked as depression, frustrations at work or home, unhappiness in relationships, their feelings can be expressed in requests like this one: "Give me perspective and help me find more joy and meaning in my days."

Though Joan was only twenty-eight years old, she looked worn down and far older. When she first came to see me, she said she was stuck ---- forever picking men who weren't there for her. "What am I doing wrong?" she asked. "No matter how much I try, they all eventually lose interest and leave."

And so we began to dig and delve together ---- moving back and forth from scrutinizing her current life to exploring her childhood. Sessions were sometimes punctuated by doubts about whether she could really change, whether I could help her, and whether therapy was worth the effort and money. But she persisted, and we plodded on.

Growing up, she had experienced more than her share of losses. When she was three years old, her father walked out, and only rarely and briefly saw her afterwards. Her mother went into a deep depression around this time. A large part of Joan's early care was taken over by a grandmother, whom she remembered as warm, but who died when Joan was six years old.

Two years after the death of her grandmother, Joan's mother's depression lifted somewhat. Her mother then met and married a man ten years older; he became a negative factor in Joan's life. Childlike and irresponsible, he drank heavily and on several occasions, made inappropriate overtures toward Joan ---- all of which ended when she turned thirteen and was able to better stand up to him. From then on, there was much tension in the family ---- daily heated arguments between her mother and stepfather and kind of an armed truce between Joan and her stepfather. In addition, mother and daughter formed an alliance: Joan offered her mother companionship in exchange for minimal nurturing.

Leaving home right after high school, Joan worked and put herself through college on a part-time basis and later went on to graduate school. Over the years, she visited her parents every few months and communicated regularly by phone with her mother. For Joan, the visits were draining and the phone calls obligatory, but she felt guilty if she didn't regularly keep in touch. She was also aware of her own fear of letting go: "As much as my mother and stepfather pull me down, they're all I have ---- especially my mother."

Together we worked hard to help Joan see her parents as people ---- their own childhoods, their dreams and fears, their strengths and weaknesses ---- and how growing up, she had coped the best she could with the situation. At the same time, we examined ways in which the men she chose now were replicas of people from her past ---- limited and not strong enough ---- and her constant surprise and hurt at the predictably hopeless conclusions of the relationships.

I was delighted when one day Joan walked into my office, practically skipping. She was radiant, like someone who has just fallen in love. But that wasn't the cause of her glow. After months of work, the puzzle had finally come together for her.

> *You've been pounding into my head that I have to see my family members as they really are and that the men I pick are comparably incomplete. At some level, though I knew you were right, part of me resisted like crazy. But this week, it suddenly came into focus: I have a choice. I don't need to keep hooking up with damaged people.*

These insights also allowed Joan to move beyond the anger she felt toward her family. Though she developed some real compassion for her mother, she chose to have much less interaction with her.

A short time after this momentous day, Joan terminated therapy. Several years later, I received a happy card saying that she had met "Mr. Right" and was getting married, and "...thanks for not giving up on me when I was so stubborn."

Not everyone has Joan's inner strength, but many, many people do have it ---- often without realizing it. I'm betting that you do!

* * *

All childhood stories should have happy endings, though. So, whether you write or not, for those of you will never hear the affirming reply you've longed for from your parents, let me offer the following letter on behalf of the parents who can't...or won't:

Dear Loved One,

While you were growing up, we wish we had been able to be better parents, to help you feel good about yourself, and to feel strong and secure inside. Unfortunately, at times we were preoccupied with our own problems ---- our relationship to each other, dealing with relatives, worries about money, work, and so on. We may have looked like adults to you, but underneath, we were scared children, much more frail and flawed than you ever imagined. We had trouble giving you "roots" and "wings" because we were often still searching for our own.

You may have felt that you didn't get the love you needed because you weren't good enough or smart enough or attractive enough or clever enough. No, none of these were true. You must stop blaming yourself for not getting what you rightly deserved ---- just because you were our child.

We also had difficulty letting you be separate from us and frequently confused your needs with ours: At times we pushed you to fill in for what we weren't, instead of being aware of who you were. Or we kept you distant when it was we who needed space, but you who really needed hugging and closeness. Or we kept you too close when we felt lost, even though you needed space. Or we weren't tuned in to what you needed at all.

That's why we're writing you now, to tell you things we wish we had told you long ago and offer you the support that we should have offered you then.

When you were little, a hug and a kiss and an "I love you" could give you plenty of mileage. It's a shame that we didn't give you a lot more of them. But you are bigger now, and it's not so simple. The best we can do is to stand by, believing in you while you work things out for yourself. And we know you have the strength to do this. Nothing would satisfy us more than to see you find inner peace and fulfillment so that you can fly on your own.

In spite of our muddled parenting, may you remember the good things, the memories we forever treasure. And whatever we didn't or couldn't share with you, we hope you will share with others in your life and with your children if you have them.

No matter what you do or who you are with, you will always be special to us, whether we stay in close contact or not. In every way we are so proud of you. Take care of yourself.

We love you very much,
Mom and Dad

Laying the past to rest is not easy. If your parents ever write this letter or any pieces of it, it will be a bonus ---- but not essential. For your growth is not contingent upon your parents' approval or their "seeing the light." Your growth depends only on you.

• *Take charge of your life now and move on.* Nurture yourself, develop a supportive human network. Do with others what was never done for and with you. (More to follow about this subject.)

Yesterday cannot be altered. Today can. And it will affect all your tomorrows.

PART II. ACCEPT THE REALITY OF WHAT IS:

Even Italians Must Stand In Line

> *Wherever you go, there you are.*
> ---- Bumper sticker

While growing up I secretly harbored the fantasy that somehow I was special, and that fact would readily be apparent to everyone who met me. I shouldn't have to wait in line, fill out endless forms for taxes, passports, or job applications. And if I were upset or overwhelmed, other people would read my mind, drop whatever they were doing and immediately come to my rescue. Since I'm a good person, that's the least they could do.

As may be true for you, I was ill-prepared for life in the real lane: Day-to-day hurdles and occasional catastrophes occur; cars and appliances break down; viable relationships require time and energy; husbands and other friends have their own agenda; children don't run like clockwork.

Wisdom about life presents itself in unlikely places. A number of years ago, as I impatiently waited in line at a money exchange in Rome, a small sign caught my eye: *"Gli italiani possono mettersi in fila come fanno gli altri!"* [Italians must get in line just like the others.] No, no, I shout to myself, surely there is a footnote saying that people like me can be exceptions.

I am not Italian, but I got the message. Though we are all exceptional in our own ways, there are no exceptions. To be adult means
- to stay in touch with who we are and where we are going;
- to feel our feelings and communicate our needs to others;
- to keep on top of life's clutter; be on call for jury duty;
- to find meaningful work, affordable housing, friends, possibly a loving mate;
- to decide who should put out the garbage;
- to accept losses related to jobs, youth, and health; and
- to maintain hope, perspective and realistic expectations about ourselves and the world at large.

And that's not all!
- Old insecurities never die;
- Bad things happen;
- Emotionally limited individuals pop up everywhere;
- Villains don't necessarily wear black; and
- When death steals loved ones, it's always too soon.

Though unpleasant topics indeed, these negative subjects kept tapping on my shoulder, insisting on having a place in any book filled with "reflections on life in the real lane." Frankly, I wanted to leave them out. But they were emphatic, claiming that unless my readers and I faced and dealt with them squarely, they would forever cause needless suffering. I replied that if they were too central to the book, you would become depressed. After a heated argument between us — many angry remarks thrown back and forth — the negatives and I finally reached a compromise. I said that they could reveal themselves fully in Part II if they promised to make nothing more than cameo appearances in the rest of the book.

The next five chapters are heavy. But you can handle them, and I'll give you some more help later.

FIVE

Old Insecurities Never Die ----
They Don't Even Fade Away

This is a test. Had it been a real life
you would have been shown where to go and what to do.
---- Bumper sticker

The successes you achieve and happiness you find as an adult cannot completely obliterate old childhood insecurities. They may lie dormant, out of sight and mind, but reappear in certain situations, particularly when you feel unusually helpless or inexperienced. At such times, much to your horror, the old insecurities return in full bloom, waving their ugly heads. You can easily revert back to feeling like the child you used to be ---- insecure, not good enough, dependent on others to make decisions for you, scared.

Any of the following situations may push your vulnerable spots:

• attending social gatherings where you don't know anyone
• being left out of group plans
• asking someone for a date
• going out on a first date
• going to a new place and getting lost

- being among others and finding you're the least capable at some activity such as dancing, sports, acting, singing or playing an instrument
- giving a speech, especially if you have little experience
- visiting in a foreign country but not knowing enough of the language to get along
  - anxiety-provoking work-related situations
    - interviewing for a job
    - asking for a raise
    - not getting a raise that you've asked for
    - being criticized by your boss
    - getting fired
  - being bawled out by an authority figure
  - getting audited
  - being cross-examined by a lawyer

* * *

As secure as I usually feel, when the going gets tough, I am always humbled and disappointed to have some of my old insecurities resurface as they did in three different situations. Let me take you back a few years when the going did get tough for me.

Legal Encounters — My Least Favorite Pastime

Over a cup of coffee, a social worker-friend for whom I consult mentions that I may be contacted by a lawyer about a client of hers whom I had seen once, two-and-a-half years ago. The case is coming up for trial in the near future. Anybody who has ever been involved with this client can be subpoenaed for a deposition.

My instant physical response to the word "lawyer" is a tightening in my gut. Lawyers are fine as friends or patients, but I hate them when they're given the power to interrupt my life and interrogate me in a third-degree deposition — more accurately, an "inquisition."

A week or so later, a message left with my answering service says that a lawyer has called. I assume that the other shoe has now dropped. Not quite yet, it turns out. The call is from the attorney for the client, informing me that I'll soon be hearing from the prosecuting attorney about setting up the deposition.

When I phone back, in many unprintable four-letter words I explain to the "good" attorney that (a) I had taken no notes ---- a habit of mine since Daniel Ellsberg's psychiatrist's confidential files were illegally raided in Washington, DC in the 1970's; (b) I have deadlines for other projects and a full load of patients; (c) I simply have no use for disrupting my schedule with this deposition; and (d) I have nothing to say anyway. The kind attorney is not blown away by my wrath and remains sympathetic and helpful to, and supportive of, this rather hysterical psychiatrist.

As the days go by, I try to forget the whole thing. It doesn't forget me. The prosecuting attorney's secretary calls. She accepts one of the possible dates I offer and agrees that the "imposition" will take place in my office (only because I'll charge an outrageously high fee if I have to go to the attorney's office). After she hangs up, I kick myself; I should have asked for a higher office fee ---- my personal suffering should be properly compensated. Several days later, a messenger materializes out of nowhere, delivers the official deposition notice, and then evaporates into the day, leaving me reeling.

The following twenty-eight-day countdown to the scheduled morning of the deposition feels awful, full of sleepless nights, though in hindsight this experience is funny.

When I get together with the social worker-friend ---- the one who has gotten me into this spot ---- for our monthly meeting about her clients, I ask about her experience with her recent deposition. She tells me it was grueling and felt endless. She learned only afterward that she could have taken breaks whenever she wanted! There had been comedy relief, however, when the slightly disheveled interrogating attorney lost the key to the bathroom and became somewhat flustered.

Since I am feeling so tense about my upcoming deposition, the usually enjoyable consultation exhausts me. I tell my friend a not-funny joke about the difference between therapists and lawyers: "Therapists have integrity and try to help people feel better; lawyers have no integrity and try to make people feel worse."

Each day my paranoia grows, my mental rehearsals become more dramatic, and my sleep becomes more fitful. Though I don't have much grey hair, I make a point of not covering it with the brown wash I normally use. I hope a little grey hair will make me look more dignified. I also update my curriculum vitae with impressive looking details.

I get together with a psychiatrist-friend and tell her my fantasy defense: to aggressively analyze out loud the opposing lawyer's emotional defenses; to observe how lucky she is that there's no key for my bathroom to lose; and if asked about the nature of my discussion with the social worker, to tell my joke about the difference between therapists and lawyers. My psychiatrist-friend laughs but tells me these are bad ideas. Any attempt to out-lawyer a lawyer could easily work against me. Instead she suggests that I take time after each question and look thoughtful. Then, depending on the complexity of the questions, before I respond, I should imagine counting huge elephants walking in a very dignified manner.

It is the day of the deposition. A little grey has reappeared in my hair. I'm dressed very conservatively, the only hint of the real me, a well-hidden frilly slip. When the doorbell rings fifteen minutes before the appointed hour, I expect the "good" lawyer to appear. Not so. It is the "other" lawyer, a woman, casual and friendly, who does not appear to be very lawyer-like. I take her friendliness to be a guise to put me off guard. So I put on a cold, distant, guarded, unfriendly stance ---- not easy to do because it goes against my personal and professional grain of liking to make other people feel comfortable. I nervously drink my coffee and offer none to her. In my fantasy, I am already well into playing my role in the courtroom melodrama even though the show has not yet started.

Another ring. It is the "good" lawyer, seven months pregnant and quite young. The two lawyers banter easily together, like old friends, about schedules, who went where to school ---- the "good" lawyer to Columbia, the "other one" to Hastings (University of California). They pay little attention to me, though in a calculated way I weave in a word edgewise about how lucky they are: "A lawyer's training is so much shorter than a psychiatrist's!" A bit of rank is established.

The appointed hour ---- nine o'clock ---- arrives and passes, but no court reporter appears. The "other" lawyer asks for and uses the phone and learns that the court reporter has had a flat tire. Twenty more minutes pass. The court reporter finally arrives, also seven months pregnant. The path to the bathroom is well used before we even begin.

When the deposition finally gets under way, the surrealistic drama unfolds ---- surrealistic because those who had up until now been human beings suddenly metamorphose into stiff cardboard characters, each playing carefully rehearsed roles. Time seems endless, but the deposition really lasts only two-and-a-half hours. During breaks I make phone calls and wander around, reminding myself that I am a physician and a mother with nothing to hide. As we file in and out of the bathroom, we again become normal human beings. These changing roles continue to make the whole experience bizarre.

I keep expecting the worst, but nothing terrible happens. Is it the impressiveness of my curriculum vitae? Is it the welcome and distracting phone calls that help me maintain my perspective? Is it because I saw the patient only once? Maybe it's the thoughtful expression on my face as I count elephants and reply in a Ronald Reagan-like style ---- "I have no recollection of details." Or it could be just good karma that day. Before I know it, the deposition is finished. The lawyers and court reporter get up to leave, and we say cordial good-byes.

What a morning! A patient's welfare has been affected by a bunch of women playing roles in a Kafkaesque drama. Not my cup of tea. I am greatly relieved: I no longer have to use my checker-playing skills in a chess game I clearly don't understand.

And why was I so worried? While I quietly reassure myself that I will never again make such a large, anxious mountain out of a nothing-but-a-nuisance molehill, part of me knows better. This is not the first or the last time I will be so thrown off stride.

I Think I May Go Crazy

I ask my husband if he can help me transfer a file from a floppy disk onto the hard disk. Being a novice with the word processor, at times I throw myself on his mercy for help. As usual, soon after I ask, he stops what he is doing and comes downstairs to help me.

"Why don't you take more notes?" my husband says. "Then you could do this yourself." I lamely remind him how much I have already learned on the word processor, how I rarely need his help now, and most of the time I can do it on my own. Inside, though, I feel like screaming.

"Okay. Sit down and write this out for yourself. Then you'll know how to do it next time."

Dutifully I sit and write: "Open Word file. Transfer in disk..."

I feel like I'm eight years old, helping my parents put away groceries in the kitchen, often in the wrong place. No one realized how hard I was trying ---- my husband doesn't realize how hard I am trying. I struggle to remind myself that I am not eight, that my husband is not my father or my mother. "Patience, Carla," I say to myself.

I still want to scream. I count to ten. I breathe deeply. We transfer the files onto the hard disk, check them out. The process feels like it takes forever. The files are coming out right. "Patience," I tell myself again. Finally the job is done. We can close down the computer. I have not screamed. I have not gone crazy. I thank my husband.

I am all right. Life is all right. I have had a temporary out-of-sanity experience and am back to my normal neurotic self.

Play Ball!

Mitts, ball, and bat in car, I pick up Mario from middle school. After stopping to share a giant roast beef submarine sandwich at a small cafe, off we go to find an open field in which to practice. It's a scene replayed on many spring days throughout the United States by countless parents and children. We throw the ball back and forth, slowly widening the distance between us. Then Mario bats and I chase balls hither and yon. Soon I take my turn at bat, hitting a few, missing a lot. Passers-by stop to stare, smiling ---- I assume ---- about the lengths a devoted mom will go to help her son improve his game.

If they listen closely, however, they will learn that it is not the mom who is helping the son, but the other way around. In other circumstances a very "teen-agish" teenager, Mario has metamorphosed into a supportive, helpful, tactful young man: "Hold the mitt right in front of your face, Mom" or "Good hit, Mom, just follow through." I get to see a lovely mature side of my son I knew must be blooming somewhere within. That's the good news. The bad news is that I'm so anxious about whether I can play softball well enough, I'm not sure I'm having fun.

A number of weeks ago I took a brave ---- and perhaps foolish ---- step and signed up with a softball team. I'd enjoyed the sport eons ago and thought I would play again "someday" when there was more time, when I wasn't so stretched juggling marriage, parenthood, and work. Time keeps passing and I'm not getting any less stretched. So, I reasoned, if not now, when? It's time to make the move, I thought, before I am old and brittle beyond redemption. Is playing softball merely a silly fantasy, a midlife minicrisis, a ridiculous attempt to turn the clock backwards, or what? Who knows?

Having gone through my local "softball connections," I hear of a team short on women, "though all the players may be eighteen years old," my friend John tells me. I leave my name on the answering machine of an unknown man with whom I trust my fate. He doesn't return any of my calls. All right, I gave it a try. Perhaps during the official spring season, I'll again build up courage and find a Park and Rec city team. After making a bona fide effort, I am at peace with my attempt and only feel a little sheepish for troubling John to get softball information for me.

But a few days later the phone rings. A strange, kind voice instructs me to appear the following Saturday morning at 9:00

A.M. at a specific field: "No need to practice beforehand. People arrive five to ten minutes ahead of game time at best."

I arrive a half hour early. After all, I rationalize, I don't know how long the drive will take, how far away I'll have to park the car, or how much time before I'll find my teammates. Well, yes, there are a couple of other reasons for not showing up anywhere near the last minute, such as my mounting anxiety about whether I can play well enough and my basic neurotic need never to be late.

Except for occasional games at picnics, I haven't played softball since high school. My mind returns to those days when I was only a bit older than my son is now. Insecurities were my constant companions during those growing-up years, insecurities which I assumed were long gone. Not so. To my chagrin, years lived, degrees earned, marriage, motherhood times four, patients helped, even my own therapy ---- none of these adult achievements insulate me from those old feelings ---- being lonely, an outsider, not okay ---- feelings never offset by good grades and the coaching of an older brother.

Our team slowly comes together. Though not eighteen years old, the players are not much older. The scarcity of women and the need to have an equal number of women and men, however, means that I am not odd woman out, one of my many anxieties. This is a good start which in part compensates for my far-from-spectacular playing.

Today we play two games. Though I don't strike out, I don't get on base either. All of my line drives are easily fielded by our nimble opponents. But I am learning ---- boy, am I learning. Having never officially played in a high pitch game, I learn to patiently "wait for my pitch." In the field I learn to play in close for women batters, far out for the men. As catcher I learn that I must put my mitt down rather than up, as I did back in high school, and that a large ball is used for men and a small one for women. And to my delight, because of such a shortage of women, in a third game between two other teams, I'm asked to join so that they won't have to forfeit. Hey, I'm needed! In this last game one of my hits not only gets me on base but breaks a tie. I'm on my way. Piece of cake!

Another Saturday rolls around. I wish I looked forward to the game without such mixed feelings. Yes, I enjoy playing: the tension of waiting in the field for a ball that may come my way, completely losing myself in the moment; teamwork; times at bat when it is up to me to "be all I can be." But I must also fight to shut out old voices in my head ---- "Don't miss" and "You have got to hit a good one" and "Don't make a fool of yourself" ---- familiar pressures from long ago.

After missing two flies in the outfield, I am temporarily replaced by a blond half my age who has a magnet in her glove. I sit on the bench ---- alone, looking like an adult, feeling like the small child I used to be. No one knows who I am or what I do, only that I am a middle-aged woman who has just missed two fly balls. Part of me wants subtly ---- or not so subtly ---- to tell them, "Hey, I'm a mother of four. I'm a psychiatrist. I'm a talk-show host. Don't discount me." As naked and alone as I feel, however, I have always looked down on those who hide behind their titles. Instead, I just wait quietly, hoping that next time I can hit the ball better or make a good enough catch so that I will temporarily be accepted ---- something the little girl in me longs for.

I wish I could say that under Mario's expert tutelage and advice (from years of Little League and tournament play), I have gone on to be a phenomenal ball player and that people say, "Look at that woman. She is older than the rest but wow can she play ball!" Not so. Two weeks ago, however, I got on first base and was surprised when everyone suddenly left the field. Only then did I realize I had driven in the winning run, ending the game. It made my week.

In the 1988 Olympics, "Eddy the Eagle" was England's only entrant in the ski-jump event. After all, with no mountains in England to practice on, can anyone blame him for not even remotely being in the league with other contenders? I remember Eddy, however, and I've forgotten the rest. When other participants bragged that "I'm going for a world record" or "I'm going for an Olympic record," Eddy the Eagle modestly proclaimed, "I'm going for survival." Well, I'm going for not making too much of a fool of myself.

Batter up!

* * *

I'm sure you have comparable tales to tell about experiences in the dentist's chair, a new class, a first meeting with your prospective in-laws, or some other difficult situation. Although we all are haunted by childhood insecurities, these periods may be more troublesome if childhood was unusually traumatic, emotionally or physically. Furthermore, people in your life now may step extra hard on your vulnerable spots if they replicate abusive or unresponsive parental figures from the past. For example, during a trying time, an uppity boss, snooty office colleagues, busy friends with no time for you, or a spouse who teases you for being afraid may topple you from your adult foundation.

The next chapter will suggest some ways to get back on your feet when life trips you up.

SIX

Bad Things Happen
Bad Wars, Bad Bosses,
Bad Neighbors...

With all its sham, drudgery and broken dreams,
it is still a beautiful world. Be careful. Strive to be happy.

---- Desiderata 1692

The new patient was early for his appointment. I asked, "Would you like to read the newspaper while you wait?" "No," he quickly answered, "I'm depressed enough already." He had a point. If we allow ourselves to dwell on all the bad things that keep happening in life, it is enough to depress anyone.

* * *

Nineteen ninety-one was a year filled with painful realities of a more or less serious nature. On January 3, while skiing at our family's favorite mountain, I get on the ski lift and after a few moments realize that Mario missed getting on with me. Immediately trying to get off to join him on the next chair, I catch my pole on the chair, twisting and fracturing my wrist. At the emergency station, I laugh about one of the questions on their standard questionnaire: Could this accident have been prevented?" Foolish question. What accident couldn't

72

be prevented? (Maybe the question is there to lift the victim's spirits.)

Okay, so the year starts with my right arm in a cast. Within a week I'm more proficient with my left hand, can drive our automatic station wagon, write at a level slightly above illegible, and still participate with Andrea in the aerobics class we had already signed up for together.

But then life takes a more serious turn.

On January 15, Mario's basketball team, made up of thirteen- and fourteen-year-old boys, is being badly beaten in a practice game. The other team is taller and outplaying ours. Usually intent on the game, my mind is miles away today. Minutes ago I've learned that after six months of trying to negotiate in the Middle East, the United Nations has declared war on Iraq.

Someone at the gym has brought a television set into the stands. I move over to watch but can barely focus on the faces on the screen. I try to sort out my feelings ---- shock, fear, but mostly an overwhelming sadness. Many of the soldiers are but a few years older than my son. Unlike after a basketball game, however, these young men won't simply pack up their shoes and uniforms for the next game. They'll leave the battleground unalterably changed ---- emotionally and/or physically scarred. Some will never go home.

In many areas, civilization has come far. But when war is waged, injuries are just as terrible and people are just as dead as they have been since the beginning of time. These soldiers are so young, in the midst of following their dreams and planning for the realities of adulthood. Thank goodness Mario is only thirteen and our other children are girls, still immune to present-day draft laws. Several friends' children are not so lucky.

As the weeks go on, I become increasingly disturbed by one realization: The combination of vileness and advanced technology can destroy life as we know it. In addition to all the humans Saddam Hussein snuffs out, it is unbelievably horrifying to watch the callous way in which he demolishes the environment, dumping oil into the gulf with complete disregard for the natural habitat and setting countless oil refineries on fire. It is always a shock to see evil so naked.

The fairy tales are right: The world contains sinister beings who have no interest in or capacity to care for the good folk. Lots of fine people are swallowed up in the havoc these "bad" people create. Brave princes don't necessarily appear in time to slay the dragons. It's scary to face life without illusions.

Strangers on the street and in stores share their fears. Good ideas emerge, such as not to watch the news right before going to bed and to see movies for distraction. A twelve-year-old patient writes about his worries: "I am trying hard, but all is not well. My brother is in the Persian Gulf. My father still drinks. My parents still fight. We are at war. All is not well."

(As I was growing up, this was not the sort of world I had in mind!)

In March, I am diverted from my preoccupation with the war: A close friend has a lump in her breast and has been advised to have a mastectomy. I urge her to get a second opinion. The second expert says that everything is fine; she only need come back for a checkup in a year. I remember the same reassuring advice resulted in the actress Ingrid Bergman's death because she did not get necessary medical care. A third consultant recommends a biopsy, which discloses a small, nonmalignant tumor. Thank God.

The ins and outs and ups and downs of daily life at home, in work, and for my family and friends continue. On March 24, after a number of visits to an orthopedist at too high a cost ---- the medical insurance covers little ---- my cast is off. Though the wrist is stiffer than anticipated and causes me quite a bit of pain, with a brace I can again ski or engage in any other shenanigans that suit my fancy.

April 25, as suddenly as the war began, it's over. I seek comfort in the notion that goodness has triumphed again ---- I guess ---- but my denial that wickedness exists is shaken and my sense of safety shattered.

* * *

As a grown-up, once you begin to hit your stride, you want to believe that with enough preplanning and ingenuity, you'll be able to outsmart and overcome all unforeseen obstacles ---- humanmade or natural disasters such as earthquakes, hurricanes and wars, mean and/or incompetent people, your own illness or that of a loved one, or other personal misfortunes. You don't want to accept the reality that bad circumstances come everyone's way and that you can sometimes do something about them and other times you can do little or nothing.

Dishonest politicians pretend to have principles and sweet-talk their way into being elected. Once in office, they may not care a whit for the land or the people they govern. On an everyday level, being qualified for a job or a promotion doesn't mean you'll get it, or if you do, that you'll be immune to layoffs no matter how many devoted years you've put in. Your work may not be properly appreciated or rewarded because your immediate superior, as Dr. Lawrence J. Peter so aptly stated in *The Peter Principle*, has risen to his or her "level of incompetence." Dr. Peter further noted that although cream rises to the top, all too often it keeps rising until it sours. Many of us get stuck with sour cream for a boss.

One of the many arts of mental health is not to allow bad "things" to reopen old wounds ---- old anxieties and insecurities. It's devastating enough to work with a difficult boss who treats you abominably or lose a job or relationship without thinking the situation is all your fault because you feel you're essentially no good.

Even for the strong and hearty, however, when life's pressures mount, your inner strength can become depleted. As a result, trying circumstances may tip you into specific psychological patterns (such as anxiety, confusion, depression, paranoia, overdrinking, overeating, or indulging in other compulsive habits) or medical conditions (such as susceptibility to colds, ulcers, high blood pressure, heart attacks, diabetes, asthma).

Stresses are like water in a lake. When they get too high, they flow over the dam ---- a dam composed of your inner and outer resources ---- and pour out into pre-established ruts, emotional and/or physical.

Incidentally, symptoms can be blatant or subtle. In a difficult work or personal situation, you may become observably upset or sick, or you might just find yourself feeling somewhat "down in the dumps" ---- "Everything is so much effort and nothing feels like fun." You need to be aware of these subtle changes.

To regain your physical and mental health, you must move away from seeing yourself as a passive victim. You must find ways to lower life stresses, increase your inner fortitude, and treat specific symptoms influenced by your inherited predisposition. The rest of this chapter offers some ways that have helped others.

• *Assess how a situation is affecting you ---- physically and emotionally.* Have you been more prone to illness or had difficulty shaking a cold or infection? Have your sleep or eating habits changed? Is every day an effort to get up and get going? Is it harder to make decisions, concentrate, remember? Do you find yourself losing touch with friends? Has the joy gone out of your life, replaced by a feeling of "what's the point of it all"?

- *Refuel and nurture yourself.* Whether you have an emotional or physical reaction, not only minister to specific symptoms with appropriate treatment, but take care of yourself as you would a friend. Cut down on your workload, screen out activities which are draining you, kick back for a few hours or days, get more sleep, and tell everyone in your life that you need plenty of TLC (tender loving care).

- *Take time to regroup.* Joel kept his emotional balance during a painful life transition in an imaginative way. His children were grown, his thirty-three-year marriage had just ended, he was burned out at work, and he was depressed. Feeling guilty about and responsible for the break up of his family, he was overwhelmed and unsure about what to do next. He decided to drive down the coast, from his home in Seattle to Santa Barbara, a place full of memories where he had attended college.

While driving south, he planned to curse the world and wallow in his pain like a small child. He would feel extremely sorry for himself only until he arrived in Santa Barbara for his visit with friends. On the return, he'd focus his energy positively, seeing other people and circumstances realistically. Based on this experience, he would figure out what direction to take in life. Joel's "coastal retreat" ---- taking time to regroup ---- turned out to be immensely helpful to him.

When life is unfair, you have a choice: Give up or go on. The only viable approach is

- to appraise what is lost and impossible to change;
- to allow yourself to feel terrible about what has happened;
- to think through potential new directions and the ramifications of each; (Giving up, staying drunk or killing yourself are not options!)
- to move on and put your energy into what is possible.

- *Write in a personal journal.* Pen and paper are always available and the price is right!

Max, an experienced teacher, was trying to mentally survive daily life with a dreadful new principal. Lester constantly undermined Max's plans for his classes, criticized him in front of fellow teachers and even students, and in many petty ways made his life miserable. Raised by an autocratic and domineering father, Max expressed his thoughts and feelings in a journal to remind himself that Lester was not his father.

> *This guy drives me nuts. He thinks he knows it all and is obviously trying to be a big shot. He talks down to me and always wants to be in control. He makes me feel like a child who is not good enough ---- like I'm doing something wrong, like I'm dependent on him to tell me what's right. I know my anxiety is way out of proportion. What's the worst he could do? Fire me? Change my program? He probably wouldn't be able to do either.*
>
> *From the grapevine I hear that he was a not-very-good teacher before he became a not-very-good principal. He's probably jealous of me and my popularity with students and other teachers at the school. In fact, when I look squarely at Lester and his track record, I can see that he is an inadequate jerk, incapable of caring about anyone's feelings but his own. I refuse to give him so much power over my life.*

When you write, don't edit; just let your thoughts flow. Getting ideas out of your head and onto paper is an effective means to help you step back to become more detached from a situation. (Incidentally, save your writings. I once asked a successful fiction writer how much of his material was autobiographical. He looked thoughtful, pondered a few moments, and answered, "Probably not more than ninety-seven percent.")

- *Develop ---- and use ---- your support system of friends.*

When your world feels upside down, these helpers validate your reality and offer useful insights, concrete suggestions, and humor. You can detoxify painful experiences by recounting them to caring people. Life can be unkind. Don't weather it alone unnecessarily.

Even acquaintances can restore your perspective. An offensive neighbor ---- a well-educated woman in her fifties, unlike good wine, grows more irritating each passing year. With one annoying gesture after another, she "endears" herself to us ---- leaving her recyclables near our doorstep and being rude to our children, among others. Over time we have grown ---- or shrunk ---- to handle the situation. We don't talk to her at all. But she still finds ways to get under our skin!

Happily the neighbor on the other side is a complete contrast. Now a man in his sixties, he was injured in a tragic motorcycle accident when he was twenty-three, resulting in left-brain damage, loss of speech, paralysis of his right arm, and limited use of his right leg. In spite of these physical limitations, however, he waves to all our family members, remembers our children with small gifts on Hallowe'en and Christmas, and forever sweeps up the leaves on his own and neighboring sidewalks.

One day as I stood near our front door talking to a friend, our gauche neighbor hosed all the dirt in front of her house down to ours, creating a giant brown mud pile of leaves and dirt near my feet. A few minutes later, seeing my dismayed look as I stood wondering what to do, our compassionate neighbor handed me a rose from his garden ---- and instantly re-established my faith in humanity.

- *Reflect on ways that other people's problems play into your own difficulties.* Through extensive personal research with friends and patients over many years, I concluded that a minimum of one out of every five people is a royal pain-in-the-neck in any given work situation. (Are you surprised about this finding?) In unusual cases, the odds are better. More often, unfortunately, they are worse. Oh, occasionally you can replace or bypass such people, and once in a blue moon you can avoid being a target for their problems by shoring up their shaky egos. This is the exception, however.

As part of my internship I worked in the busy emergency room of a hospital in Cleveland. On a particularly hectic day, I was diligently trying to close a woman's bleeding leg wound. The stitching was hard enough, but my task was made far more difficult by the rude, inappropriate comments of a hospital administrator who unexpectedly dropped by.

Sensing I was upset, Lucille, a wise nurse, took me aside and mentioned that this man's obnoxious behavior was probably a "macho" cover-up for his uneasiness about seeing so much blood. She suggested I attempt to reassure him. So I commented casually that it's perfectly normal to be frightened of blood and that working in a hospital doesn't automatically banish these fears. The administrator quieted down, and I was able to finish my stitch work. He even complimented me graciously.

Such tactics succeed when the other person is essentially sensitive but treats others badly as a defense against personal insecurities or problems. Not all individuals respond as readily, of course. Your most useful tool is to learn how to avoid taking an offender's remarks personally.

• *Find healthy ways to maintain your equilibrium in unhealthy situations.* Get beyond frustration, disappointment, and anger so these feelings don't devour you.

Jeannette was furious at an obnoxious coworker who forever slammed the door loudly. She had already spoken to this man and his superior, but the rude behavior continued. She liked her job and didn't want to quit, but she felt helpless.

I knew that Jeannette was a talented amateur artist, so I told her a story I had heard about Diego Rivera, who had painted Lenin into a magnificent mural for Rockefeller. Rockefeller, however, felt that the mural was far too Communist-leaning for his taste and had it replaced. Diego Rivera was livid about Rockefeller's actions but handled his anger in a unique way. He later recreated the mural in the Palacio de Belles Artes in Mexico City, painting partying women near the figure of Rockefeller and syphilis bacilli over Rockefeller's head.

When I next saw Jeannette, she smiled and showed me a fine painting of an ugly man with a large door slammed directly into his face.

Don't dismiss revenge fantasies because you think they're moronic or downright sinful. On the contrary, if someone has wronged you, thoughts of sending that person into permanent orbit in outer space can give you a good night's sleep and restore your mental health. (Where do you think science fiction and mystery writers get ideas for their stories?)

To keep my sanity, when I was working for an extremely manipulative and intrusive boss, I wrote the following limerick and gleefully shared it with friends:

Seen as a "joke" without tact,
Good judgement she certainly lacked,
A pain in the ass,
Immature and quite crass,
Not soon enough will she be sacked.

You may think this is a childish approach to life, but as a result of my "limerick therapy," I was able to put this boss into the background and started enjoying work again. (Postscript: *I* actually got sacked first!)

Caught in a traffic jam, you have a choice. You can fume and raise your blood pressure or relax and listen to good music. It is a waste of life to stay upset.

- *When a situation allows, stand up and be counted.* It's not always possible to give guilty parties their due. In many bad circumstances, reality, physical danger, the possibility of law suits (or sometimes just good manners) prevent you from making things right. Whenever possible, however, it feels good to speak your mind.

As Mario and I waited in line to order a sandwich at one of our favorite quick-stop restaurants, a tall, severe looking woman left her table in the dining area and announced, to no one in particular, "Someone should clear the tables. They are full of crumbs. No decent person can eat there." Several minutes later she marched up again, waving her sourdough loaf sandwich, and declared to another customer in line, "I hope yours isn't burned like this!" Then turning to the short-order cook she demanded, "Scrape off the burned part. No. I didn't say cut it off. Scrape it off. Can't you understand anything?" Then she stalked again back to her table.

When we got our food, we sat as far away from the woman as possible ---- I wish we had been farther away! As we began to talk about our experiences that day and plans for the weekend, the woman blasted us: "Can't you speak quieter? It's bothering me."

She was not a burly man. She didn't look physically fit or likely to be carrying a concealed weapon. So I became bold, much to the embarrassment of my son: "Lady, I don't know what your problem is, but if you don't like it here, why don't you go out into the street where we won't bother you?" She and I exchanged a few more choice words as Mario tried to become invisible, shrinking down in his chair. Eventually in a slightly louder voice than necessary, I continued my conversation with him.

- *If the price is too high, cut your losses.* Like throwing away good money with bad, walk away from intolerable situations ---- if you can. Toxic or not-good-enough personal or work circumstances are common. After leaving, people say, "In hindsight, I wish I'd gotten out much sooner."

Once in a while, bad individuals ---- thorns in our sides ---- move to other cities, transfer to other departments, or retire. (Not often enough, though, in my opinion!) Many years ago, my friend Myra's life became a nightmare because of her supervisor's behavior. Not only did he make sexual overtures toward her and tell unflattering lies about her to colleagues, he also passed on stories to the main boss, challenging Myra's integrity. Myra's description revealed a man without much conscience or the capacity to care about others.

After weeks of such harassment, Myra called one day in high spirits. When asked if she'd finally gotten her promotion, she gleefully replied, "No! The bum died!" Afterwards, of course, she felt more sympathetic about his death, but her first reaction was delight.

When friends or patients speak of feeling trapped in miserable marriages or unhappy work environments, I sometimes tell Myra's story. Yes, occasionally offending individuals in one way or another disappear into thin air, but it's rare. You best not count on it. So, rather than waiting for lightning to strike the hateful souls, your mental health demands that you actively remove yourself from the grievous situation on your own.

* * *

Last, but not least, don't confuse nuisances, no matter how odious, with tragedies.

Remember the story of the man who had no shoes and complained bitterly until he met someone who had no feet? A 1988 interview with Stephen W. Hawking, the disabled forty-six-year-old genius who wrote *Brief History of Time*, revealed his acceptance of life and his determination to continue to live fully despite a debilitating disease. Amyotrophic lateral sclerosis, often called Lou Gehrig's disease, had so destroyed the motor nerves of Hawking's body, he could no longer speak and remained confined to a wheelchair. Except for the ability to use his fingers to activate control buttons of his special computer, he had no way to move or communicate. Still he continued his work, advancing the science of black holes and the lives of stars and looking for an "ultimate theory": to link gravitational physics with quantum mechanics. He authored several very successful books.

At a press conference, a comparably disabled man strapped into a wheelchair asked for advice for those with degenerative illnesses. Through his computer's speaker, Hawking answered: "This is very difficult. I think one just has to try to do the best one can with the situation in which one finds oneself. I myself have been very fortunate."

SEVEN

Emotionally Limited Individuals Pop Up Everywhere

"How many psychiatrists does it take to change a light bulb?"
"You can't change a light bulb unless it really wants to change."
                    ---- Anonymous (old psychiatric riddle)

• *Several times, my husband and I had rescued Eliana from difficult situations. We loaned her money, allowed her to live at our home when she was between apartments, and offered shoulders to cry on when she was between boyfriends. We never asked anything from her in return until we needed a few hours' help in moving to our new home. She refused. "Sorry, I can't," she said to me on the phone. "Moving depresses me." We never heard from her again.*

• *We'd known Luis and Caroline for many years before they decided to get a divorce. Caroline confided to me that their eight-year-old son was having sleeping problems and their five-year-old daughter wouldn't let her mother out of sight. When I met Luis at a school function, I gently said that I was sorry these were tough times for them and wondered if there was anything I could do to help their children. With a grin that looked pasted on, he quickly declared, "We're all fine," and changed the subject.*

• *While growing up, I observed Tom, the uncle of a friend of mine. Whenever I met him, he flashed a too-broad smile and with a condescending air, asked me a stream of questions: "How have you been?" "How is school?" "How is your family?" and so on. Somehow, however, Tom neither listened to nor seemed interested in my answers. In fact, many times he started to talk about some aspect of his own life while I was still answering his last question. Although Tom remained physically present he drifted away mentally, and I was left emotionally alone. My friend and I would refer to him as "the little man who never was."*

What was it with these people? Why did they seem so distant, so uncaring, so insensitive, even cold? I began to wonder: Was it me? Something I had said or done? Or was there more to the story?

Understanding Emotionally Limited Individuals

We recognize when people have obvious limitations. Some have physical disabilities or are in wheelchairs or without limbs. Others have limits of intelligence evident in their speech or measured by standard intelligence tests. They are unable to grasp information easily, move forward in school, or learn in classic ways. We accept them, and we rejoice in their victories, however small.

But it's difficult to accept people who appear to be sound in body and mind but are deficient in vital social and emotional abilities. They may lack heart, soul, compassion, common sense, or judgement. They may be insensitive to the needs of others, like Isabel, the substitute teacher for our aerobics class. She could lift her leg higher, race through routines faster, and make more beautiful turns than any of us. We couldn't keep up. That was the problem. Out of touch with the capacities and needs of the class, Isabel appeared extremely bored and looked at the clock no less than every five minutes. When one angry class member finally told

Isabel about our general dissatisfaction with her teaching, Isabel completely missed the point. Before the next class she simply stated, "One of you mentioned you were bothered that I glanced at the clock so frequently. I want to apologize. Without my glasses I can't see my watch clearly." To no one's surprise, she continued to conduct the class in the usual way.

Some people may cross unwritten social rules, preoccupied with their own needs and abysmally unaware of acceptable social niceties in specific settings. Jerry taught Spanish at a local college, and I enrolled in his extension course. During the term, in spite of knowledge of his subject and many useful class exercises, he spent most of the time displaying his own facility for language. When he did actually interact with us, he would ration his praise and support as if painfully squeezing toothpaste from a tube. My assessment of Jerry was confirmed when we had a potluck supper at a classmate's home after the class was over. Each of us brought generous helpings of treats or hand made delicacies; Jerry appeared with a lone bottle of cheap wine.

The bottom line is this: Although such people look whole and capable, interactions with them can be frustrating and upsetting experiences.

Some people like Tom go through the motions of connecting with others, but seem detached. You may recount personal information, happy or sad, or disclose an important idea. But when you encounter them later, they make little or no reference to your previous conversation, as if it never occurred.

You assume that teachers will teach, parents will parent, and educated people will be honest and savvy about life because that's what they're supposed to do. You count on partners to be as thoughtful of you as you are of them. When life hurts, you think others will feel the way you do. And when they don't, and the offenders are not even bothered by their own callousness, you're shocked.

Why are these people emotionally unavailable and socially out of synch with the needs of those around them? Were they born this way or has life soured them?

Our old friends, nature, nurture, and fate grant most people a capacity to feel a full range of emotions and the ability to stay vulnerable and experience great intimacy with others. To most people, but not to all.

Emotionally Withdrawn Individuals. Some people are emotionally withdrawn. Having a capacity for a full range of feelings, these people appear to have shut down at some point. Jacob was a well-respected physician in our community who had lost his zest for life. He still played the piano beautifully and sometimes sketched gentle nature scenes, but there was no longer a sparkle in his eyes. Word of mouth had it that in his youth Jacob had been a real fighter, leaving first his loving but overbearing family and later, his war-torn homeland, Poland. After that, however, too much sadness pervaded his life —— the deaths of relatives in concentration camps and the death of his first wife several years after he immigrated to the United States.

By the time I knew him, he'd lost his vitality —— only the scars of his battles remained. His pain was palpable; whenever I visited him, I found myself unsuccessfully trying to cheer him up. He had so retreated within himself the last time I saw him, it was almost impossible to reach him. These changes were especially sad for me, for he was the father of my best friend.

Emotionally withdrawn people are extremely —— perhaps overly —— sensitive and feel too responsible for everyone and everything. Such people might have had unbelievably sad childhoods, full of losses, too much to bear. Their losses could have included the death of, or physical or emotional abandonment by, a key parental figure. In other instances, however, the losses might not seem that great, but at some level they overwhelmed the inner or outer resources of a given child.

These people used to be alive. They had dreams and risked being vulnerable and tender. But somewhere along the way they got worn down. A combination of accumulated frustrations, disappointments, or setbacks crushed them. As a result, they gave up on life's adventures and settled into a holding pattern of marking time and growing older, and what is so tragic, often living a minimal existence.

Emotionally withdrawn individuals are basically depressed, although the depression can be hidden. (We looked at a few examples in Chapter 2.) Substance abuse (alcohol and other drugs) or a compulsive pattern around food, money or an activity, (e.g., workaholism) may be prominent. For many such people, chronic illness or further withdrawing into the self may have closed the door permanently.

Emotionally Incomplete Individuals. Other people are emotionally incomplete and stagnate at a two-or three-year-old's self-centered level. Ray, a professor, was troubled about his wife, Karen. Over the course of a fifteen-year marriage, she spent their money freely, had numerous affairs, and appeared to feel no guilt or remorse about her actions. In addition, Karen was often away from their children, leaving them in haphazardly arranged baby-sitting situations. Since Karen was conscientious in community activities, those who didn't know her well were unaware of her irresponsible behavior.

Obvious neglect, abuse or overindulgence may be contributing causes to behavior such as Karen's. People like her may never have had the chance to relate to a caring, consistent parental figure. Or they may have been overprotected and never encouraged nor allowed to mature. At other times, however, the reason for the incomplete development remains a mystery.

Sociopathic Individuals. At the extreme, emotionally incomplete people are so *narcissistic* as to be emotionally empty. They are referred to as *sociopathic,* or as having *antisocial personalities,* with specific characteristics:

• They have no capacity for genuine feelings. Any expression of emotion is based on intellectually figuring out what is expected in a given situation, not on a gut reaction from inside.

• As in a poker game, they use others largely for personal gain. They borrow money or ask favors and conveniently "forget" to return them. They enter relationships for power or prestige and/or have children primarily for their own egos. Their interaction with others lacks depth as they are unable to understand or care deeply about anyone else's feelings. It is to be noted, however, that such individuals may function adequately in impersonal situations at work or elsewhere in the world.

Incidentally, sociopathic qualities are far more obvious in strangers than in those close to you, as we'll explore in the next chapter.

You may have experienced firsthand what happens when emotionally limited people hold positions of power. Emotionally withdrawn supervisors may be so self-absorbed that they're ineffectual leaders, unable to properly keep order. Chaos results: An organization becomes like a ship run by the crew, or the strongest bully in the crew, because the captain is asleep. Working for them can be unpleasant and downright hazardous to your mental health. Emotionally incomplete supervisors are particularly dangerous because their power is not offset by a capacity to care for others. I once had a boss who was so busy trying to get ahead in the organization that she spent no energy attending to the daily workings of our gradually deteriorating department. Sociopathic supervisors are a disaster to work for ---- lacking a conscience, they only play by their own rules.

As an employee, avoid going crazy by properly assessing your boss's limits. Otherwise, all too easily you'll fall into the rut of taking personal responsibility for the supervisor's inappropriate reactions.

It goes without saying that a blindness to people's emotional limits can be especially devastating in romantic relationships. You keep kissing frogs that fail to turn into princes and blame yourself for the lack of metamorphosis. Or you perpetually put glass slippers on too small or too big feet without noticing the slippers don't fit.

Dealing with Emotionally Limited People

The vignettes in this chapter are drawn from the lives of relatives, friends, and acquaintances of mine and of my patients. It's not by chance that these people were not patients themselves. Emotionally withdrawn individuals would rather remain in minimal lives than risk being vulnerable. Facing their feelings is too painful. Emotionally incomplete individuals are rarely aware of or bothered by their limits, and hence, only enter therapy with pressure from others and seldom stay. Sociopaths don't seek therapy because they just don't care. When forced into therapy by the courts, they rarely accomplish anything other than learning new ways to manipulate the system.

For you, however, the central question is this: Why is it so difficult to see the limits of such people and how these limits might affect you? You look for healthy reactions and don't get them. But rather than admit that the individuals in question are incapable of giving more, you assume it's your fault because:

- You're expecting too much: "She works so hard at the office, no wonder she has little patience with the children."
- Your behavior causes the inappropriate or inadequate response: "I'm such a rotten housekeeper. I'm sure that's why he pays so little attention to me."
- You're overreacting to the entire situation: "I know I'm always mad as hell when my parents put down my latest interest, but maybe I'm just being oversensitive."

In sum, you may set yourself up to be let down.

The following factors can play into your denial of people's emotional and social limits.

- It's uncomfortable to accept the fact that certain individuals are incomplete and, for all practical purposes, unavailable. You want to believe everyone has the capacity to become a full, caring human being, able to lead a fulfilling life. For instance, if you have been consistently passed over for a promotion at work, you keep hoping that more hard work can earn the promotion. You feel helpless if you have to accept the fact that your boss is a bigoted, narrow-minded person with little conscience, who plays favorites with his cronies, and that you will never get beyond your present rank.
- If a close relative is emotionally limited, particularly a parent, sibling, partner or child, giving up the illusion that everything was or can be all right is exceptionally hard. To realize that someone close to you may be irrevocably damaged is tragic and extremely disturbing.

My friend Erica is beginning to understand that her mother will never be "all right."

> *Growing up, I never could get my mother's attention. I kept trying —— working for better grades, endlessly doing little chores around the house, even getting into trouble. But I could never get her attention. Even as an adult, in her presence I find myself acting like I did when I was little —— trying harder*

and harder and getting nowhere. I don't want to see the futility of her ever being close to me ... and that she will never change.

I've not been immune to such illogical thinking.

Everything that works for me with patients ---- my desire to help, my facility to cut through small talk, my ability to push people to stop kidding themselves, my agility in getting people to ponder their dreams and ways they've sold out on themselves ---- lands me in big trouble in other settings.

When people I care about keep getting trapped in self-created disasters or, to me, seem stuck in narrow lives walled by habit and fear, I act like a God-appointed messenger whose duty is to help them see the light. Bad enough in the ordinary conversations of the day, my zeal becomes ridiculous in evenings filled with conviviality and a bit of wine or other good cheer.

In such instances, I'm quickly transformed into my psychiatric persona and jump full force into the lives of those who happen into my path, inviting the unsuspecting to look beneath the surface, to question themselves, to take responsibility for finding meaning in life and living it to full potential. "Tim, do you notice how all the women you date are so darn needy? Maybe that's why the relationships go nowhere." "Rosie, I know that looks shouldn't be so important, but don't you think your fifty-odd extra pounds would initially put a man off? Then he might not take the time to get to know what a really nice person you are."

And I never learn.

Once started, the same scenario unfolds. Temporarily Tim or Rosie or the other objects of my ministrations may have brief moments of reflection, invariably soon interrupted by some pressing reality or by the person (Tim or Rosie) or someone else nearby conveniently changing the subject to less emotionally laden issues. Then my subjects either mentally or physically leave. But I'm a die-hard optimist; I think I've made a major breakthrough to free them, to move them forward ---- toward a more fulfilling life.

Not so.

The next time we meet, Tim's or Rosie's shell has been re-erected, the defenses put firmly back in place. No one is grateful for my unrequested efforts to help. In fact if anything comes up about the previous conversation, I'm the one who's seen as too serious, too emotional, too intrusive. And me? I feel disappointed, hurt, unappreciated.

Suffice it to say,

- we need to acknowledge that there will be emotionally limited people in our lives.
    - some will be benign and some will be malignant
    - we'll care about some and some we won't
- we have to let go of attempting to change those who can't or don't want to change ---- even when they are Tims and Rosies ---- people we love.

Not all stories will have happy endings.

EIGHT

Why Don't The Villains Wear Black?

*The belief in a supernatural source of evil is not necessary,
men alone are quite capable of every wickedness.*
---- Joseph Conrad (1912)

At some time or another you've probably bought an appliance, reportedly in "perfect condition," only to discover ---- after it was fully installed in your home ---- you purchased a lemon. Or perhaps when one garage mechanic said your car needed a new carburetor or engine, you were sensible enough to take it to another garage for a second opinion and found out the carburetor or engine would run fine with minor adjustments.

Someone without principles may have used you or your ideas. Beth, a college friend, presented an innovative idea to the committee evaluating her work for a Ph.D. Later she learned that one evaluator on her committee had taken the idea and not only published it independently, but sold it commercially and made a great deal of money.

You might have lent a small or large sum of money to a "friend" who told you a phenomenal hard-luck story. Kind person that you are, you readily bought it all. And of course, your "friend" never repaid the loan. Maybe you've heard about someone ---- or possibly you have been the "someone" ---- who invested in what turned out to be a poor-risk stock, a run-down piece of property, a nonexistent gold mine, or some similar ruse. And to top it off, the helpful seller suddenly left town with no forwarding address. You may have read about, or yourself become a pawn of, a television evangelist or cult leader who mesmerized hundreds or even thousands of people, bilked them out of their money, and took over their lives.

Newspapers abound with tales of mail-order frauds, rip-off schemes, and even more vicious situations. I remember reading about a smooth-talking man who routinely passed himself off as a professional soccer player, conning soccer teams out of salary advances without any teams seeing him play. More than one story has hit the headlines about computer "hackers" who break into computers and steal credit card numbers, cellular telephone codes and company secrets.

Maybe you were sold a bill of goods by a "highly recommended" dentist and after he retired, you found out from your new dentist that all of your fine, expensive gold crowns had been completely unnecessary. Perhaps a hungry lawyer urged you to press legal charges ---- against your former dentist, for example ---- and you ended up wasting even more of your time, energy, and money while only the lawyer benefited. And I hate to mention all the unnecessary medical procedures ---- uteruses removed, back surgeries performed, and tests ordered ---- to fill empty hospital beds or underwrite yachts or vacations for unscrupulous practitioners.

Perpetrators of such crimes are often trusted people in positions of authority ---- parents or other relatives, supervisors, physicians, and others.

Adolf, a bright, articulate chemist, apparently had an on-going incestuous relationship with his niece from the time she was seven years old. This crime only came to light when, as an adult, the niece experienced severe emotional problems. Later, other family members, male and female, also acknowledged that Adolf had attempted to molest them. When confronted, Adolf first denied what he had done. But when many relatives cornered him with the facts, he replied, "Why not?" ---- with no apologies, no explanations, no remorse.

Although the niece felt too upset about the situation and too intimidated by Adolf to take legal action, a measure of justice came through an act of nature. Several years after the molestation became known, during a trip to a small town in southern Mexico, Adolf contracted cerebral malaria and fell quite ill. He was immediately hospitalized, fell into a coma, and died a week later.

There is a Spanish saying: *"La gente mala nunca muere. Y si muere, ni falta hace."* [Bad people don't die. And even if they do, no one cares."] When Adolf died, however, many relatives felt great relief and some understandably rejoiced, particularly his niece. With Adolf no longer around, the shadow he had cast over her life seemed to lift ---- at least partially. Subsequently, with the help of a great deal of therapy, she was able to get her life together.

All of these less-than-honest people are variations of sociopaths described in Chapter 7 ---- emotionally limited people who use good folk financially and in worse ways and who have little or no conscience about doing so. What's different and frightening about the truly villainous sociopaths, however, is that in varying degrees, they actively seek out their prey and enjoy their conquests.

Con artists who carefully lure their victims into handing over money are examples of such sociopaths. I often wondered what kind of people get taken in and taken by con artists ---- surely victims must be extraordinarily naive. From talks with my longtime friend George, however, I discovered how easily any of us can become victims

- if we are in times of transition or vulnerability,
- if we trustingly bend to someone who flatters us,
- if we fail to see the red flags of trouble.

And I have learned since that con artists can "smell out" such vulnerable people. But I'm getting ahead of my story.

George and I first became friends when I was in medical school, and he, in graduate school in journalism. We used to meet for coffee regularly to discuss a variety of mutual concerns. Though we brought different perspectives to our discussions about the human condition, we both prided ourselves in defending underdogs, in not being taken in by the labels society puts on particular individuals, and in seeing people's potential even when they have followed wrong paths ---- and we still do. In other words, we try to give people the benefit of the doubt.

Our careers took us in different geographic directions. I went to California; he stayed in Ohio. He's moved around a bit, but he's still in the news business after twenty years. I've kept in touch with George and his wife, Marie, by letter and phone and occasional visits.

I've always admired George's instincts as a reporter and his interest in people. And I'm not the only one. He's respected among his peers throughout the country for his integrity and honesty.

About twelve years ago, George won a major journalism award for his series about men's lives after incarceration. When he called to tell me the news, I was thrilled for him. While he was researching and writing the articles, he described face-to-face interviews with former prisoners, some living in halfway houses. Occasionally he sent drafts of particular articles and seemed to value my comments. The final series showed George's unique ability to report the facts and to reveal the human faces behind them.

Not long after George received the award, a man named Bruno sought him out to talk about the issue of individuals wrongly accused of sexually abusing children and unjustly imprisoned. Bruno had served a three-year prison term for allegedly molesting children at a child-care center and apparently blamed the director of the center for his unjust conviction.

George's series of articles had attracted Bruno, who claimed that his own trial had been unfair, that his prison experience had enabled him to gain insight into what it was like to be wrongly accused of such a hateful crime, and that he would like to help others.

George told me he was touched by Bruno's story. Though I encouraged him to ask Bruno to fill in the details about the basis for the charges against him, George insisted that Bruno's story was sound. Besides, he had come to like Bruno.

George had never had a good-enough relationship with his own father, who had died a few months earlier, and evidently found solace in his friendship with Bruno, who was fifteen years older. True, Bruno's credentials were far from impeccable ---- (and in fact were downright "peccable"). But George ---- emotionally vulnerable ---- was and is a defender of the less fortunate, a bill Bruno filled perfectly.

As George told me about Bruno in letters and phone conversations, I wondered aloud why Bruno kept after him with such a passion. "Bruno," George explained, "regularly reads my articles and thinks I am the only newspaper reporter who really fights for people's rights." Bruno inundated George and his family with phone calls, cards, and later, small gifts. His thoughtfulness, flattery and charisma (George's word) led my friend to feel quite close to Bruno.

Meanwhile, I had become more and more skeptical about what I perceived to be Bruno's superficial "goodness." In fact, the mention of Bruno's charisma raised a red flag in my mind: *Con artists are often charismatic.* I advised George to beware of someone who so instantly becomes a friend and who is persistent. But I couldn't seem to convince George to be more cautious.

Several weeks later, George decided to interview Bruno for an article about his wrongful prison experience. The article drew praise from George's editor, a number of letters from readers, and a gracious thank-you note from Bruno. Clearly Bruno had tapped into a problem for which help was needed. Subsequently his story led to radio and TV interviews, but then George became busy with other work ---- including research for a new series ---- and didn't mention Bruno for several months. I was relieved to hear that Bruno was out of George's life!

But Bruno hadn't forgotten George. Bruno surfaced again to ask if George would sit in on some meetings of a group for people unjustly incarcerated and recently released from prison. And maybe George would edit (for pay) the group's fledgling newsletter? George agreed and began working with Bruno and his group. He complained to me, however, that in spite of many requests, payments for his work never materialized. Against my advice, George let it slide because he enjoyed his contacts with Bruno, and he thought he was helping out in a "good cause."

Eventually George became annoyed with Bruno about not getting paid and began to avoid contact with Bruno.

Then out of the blue came such an opportunity that George forgot about the unpaid salary. Bruno had been invited to speak on the topic "Leading a Productive Life Following Wrongful Incarceration" at a national convention of the Social Services Society. George was asked ---- because of his

award-winning series and other journalistic achievements ----
to share the platform with Bruno. The organization would
fly them to New Orleans, put them up in a posh hotel, and
cover all expenses. I was pleased for George, but also
cautioned him again about Bruno's foibles. He was too
excited to listen: "I've never been to New Orleans ---- just the
trip alone will be great!" Most important to George, he could
share his knowledge and experience with experts who were
in a position to do something for wrongfully imprisoned
people. The chance to help them ---- even indirectly ---- was
irresistible.

Thanks to Bruno, George was starting to feel like a
celebrity. A couple of major metropolitan newspapers had
run his articles, and he was reveling in his notoriety, which
was understandable. At the same time, George kept relating
the incongruities in Bruno's life, which sounded ominous ----
gaps in his stories, strange mood swings that didn't make
sense, an endless trail of former so-called friends who
suddenly disappeared from his life, and an absence of any
relatives. I started to warn him more emphatically: "George,
watch out for this guy!" But somehow he managed to bury
thoughts about these inconsistencies and Bruno's promised
payments behind the fun he was having and the good cause
he felt he was a part of.

Bruno was in full gear. He began to form support groups
for those wrongly incarcerated, for which he told George he
needed money. George and Marie discussed at length how
much they would become involved, eventually deciding to
lend Bruno $5,000 for office supplies and staff salaries. To
reassure them, Bruno promised to incorporate and make
George and Marie shareholders. They were excited about
being in on the ground floor of a good cause and celebrated
with much champagne.

George didn't tell me about his monetary investment in Bruno's ventures until after he and Marie had already given Bruno the money. By then, I sensed Bruno's plan ---- the three G's con artists use to hook people: *Goodness, Gullibility,* and *Greed*. Though I pointed this out to George, he didn't want to see it. Besides, he and Marie had become shareholders in what they thought could become a financial windfall ---- or, at the very least, a worthwhile cause.

George was also getting another payoff from his work with Bruno: a case of "writer's block" he had experienced while working on his own novel began to evaporate. He was enthusiastic about getting his "non-newspaper" writing back in gear and rationalized that writers often were not paid their due. And as he threw himself into these new projects, for which his clever mentor gave him ample praise and encouragement, lo and behold, the sorrow which had followed his father's death started to lift as well.

I counseled George about a con artist's flattery ---- and the "false positive" feelings it creates. I suggested that these feelings would seem especially comforting to him because he was grieving his father's death and needed the compassion and reinforcement Bruno seemed to offer. George thanked me for my concern, but paid little attention to it.

When Bruno eventually told George he had used up all of his own savings and the money George and others had contributed, George and Marie loaned him additional money. Bruno thanked them profusely and treated them to dinner at a nice restaurant, saying, "It's only fair for all that you've done for me." When George admitted to me (rather sheepishly) that he'd given Bruno more money, I said, "A *dinner* in payment for a several-thousand-dollar investment??" George said he and Marie hadn't enjoyed such a nice dinner for months...

A few weeks later, George wrote me a note saying that although he and Bruno were still close, other people were beginning to complain about Bruno. The printer of the newsletter had not been paid, though George reassured him that it must have been an oversight on Bruno's part. George knew that someone had given Bruno money specifically to pay for this printing ---- and Bruno of course corroborated the "oversight" story. In addition, two members of Bruno's staff said they'd not received the salary owed them, but George assumed it was "merely a mix-up." George kept dismissing other people's doubts and finding explanations for their complaints. But I said, *"Red flag,* George, *red flag!* Check out these 'oversights'!"

My continued skepticism together with his other associates' observations, at least at some level, were causing George to grow uneasy. George told me Bruno too readily had answers that cleverly put everyone else on the defensive ---- "You mean you really think I would cheat you? I can't believe you could even have such a thought about me." And often when George and Marie tried to talk business with Bruno, he was moody and evasive.

George and Marie became increasingly distressed about the situation. Bruno offered no detailed accounting about where their money was being used and of course no payment to George for his writing and editing. When questioned, Bruno replied in what George later described as "Oscar-winning style": "I'll give you the money I owe you as soon as other money is returned to me" or "You never sent me an itemized bill" or "The bank/post office must have lost my check."

Thank goodness George and Marie's suspicions finally couldn't be quieted any longer. Researching on their own, they discovered that Bruno had never incorporated his group for those wrongly incarcerated or applied to register his organization with the state. Thus, his note to George and Marie verifying their shares in the organization was meaningless.

At last, their denial crumbled. They knew they'd been royally taken. "Why don't the villains wear black?" George half-jokingly said to me.

* * *

Looking back on the experience, George concluded (as I had already) that his personal philosophy ---- trying to give people the benefit of the doubt ---- and his father's recent death had left him more vulnerable than he realized at the time, wide open to look for comfort in all the wrong places. When Bruno came into his life, George chose *not* to see any of the warning signs or listen to the cautions of others because Bruno made him feel good. Bruno then led George and Marie to think they were helping a good cause, but in reality, they had given credibility and a respectable facade to a con artist's schemes, allowing themselves and other innocent people to be victimized. The whole experience had been sobering ---- and humbling.

When I told George I was writing a book about "life in the real lane," he invited me to tell his story in hopes of sparing others the grief that he and Marie experienced.

* * *

As I sought to further my own understanding of how my friends had been so readily duped, I came across two books that present especially enlightening discussions about sociopaths.

• *The Stranger Beside Me,* by Ann Rule, is a startling autobiographical account of her interactions with a serial killer who worked with her for several years at a suicide hotline. Like Bruno, he was able to be superficially kind and thoughtful and seemingly act with integrity toward people while at the same time grotesquely victimizing them when the opportunity arose. (Rule's protagonist, of course, murdered his victims; con artists "do them in" financially.)

• *The Mask of Sanity*, by Hervey Cleckley, M.D., is a brilliant examination of sociopaths. He describes people with superficial charm who are incapable of relating to anyone on a deep level. Such individuals use others for their own egocentric needs ---- with complete absence of remorse or shame ---- readily lying and slickly blaming to cover up their transgressions. Furthermore, sociopaths commit their crimes in a robotlike way for astonishingly small stakes and without a specific goal.

I am sad that people like Bruno exist, casualties of civilization who come from any walk of life. They might be strangers with no discernible connection to society. But they can also be neighbors, coworkers, bosses, "friends," dates, relatives, and even well-credentialed individuals masked with fancy degrees ---- M.S.W., M.D., Ph.D. They may have grown up poor or have pedigrees that grace the social registers. No matter what disguises they wear, however, they are masters at gaining your confidence, appropriating your money, or violating you in more grotesque ways.

* * *

I can only advise you

• to be cautious about someone who is too-friendly, perhaps peddles a hard-luck story, and instantly makes you feel too close, too soon, without good reason. (Be especially careful if you're going through a period of transition or loss.)

• to beware of someone who flatters you, makes you feel indispensable, and holds out to you the possibility of future fame or fortune.

• to look closely at the person's history ---- check out stories and talk to friends and past associates.

- to tune in to and trust your gut feelings if anything seems awry.

- to pay attention to the red flags that signal trouble ---- for you may have bumped into one of these unidentifiable villains who hide in the crevices and feed on the good-hearted and unsuspecting.

NINE

When Death Steals Loved Ones, It's Always Too Soon

All I know of love is that love is all there is.
---- Emily Dickinson

W hen I was little, I could in part envision my life as temporary; I was "only dancing on this earth for a short time." But I never imagined that people close to me wouldn't always be here. I don't want to accept the fact that I must die ---- that we all must die ---- and worse yet, that those I love may die before I am ready to let them go...

I don't like death. It's so damn final. For days and weeks and months after it happens, even when your mind wanders elsewhere and you temporarily forget about the death and relax, it comes back to plague you. Thoughts about it keep hitting you again and again and again; each time you feel devastated anew. And if it involves someone very special, even years later, if you allow yourself to feel the full impact of the loss, you are likely to be ripped apart inside.

As adults, although taking good care of ourselves improves our own odds, the loss of loved ones inevitably touches all of us. Sorrow hits randomly, illness strikes, accidents happen. New and long-term friends and treasured relatives can be victims.

My children are lucky. For the most part their lives have been safe and predictable. They have not gone through famines or other world catastrophes. They mourned the death of a beloved grandfather. They were saddened by the demise of two rabbits, two guinea pigs, and a rat. Many people of their generation are less fortunate; they have grown up with death being a regular visitor in their lives.

Is it possible to let yourself care deeply about others without constantly guarding against the fear of losing them? When there is a loss, how do you avoid becoming bitter or consumed by sadness?

My third grade teacher, a delightful woman who wrote poetry and played the piano with a vengeance, lived to be 104 years old. When she was still a feisty ninety-eight, I went to visit her. She told me the hardest part of living so long was that none of her contemporaries were still alive.

Each kind of loss has its own singeing pain. Loss of parents gives a finality to your growing-up years. With their passing, you lose the chroniclers of your history and no longer have a generation to buffer you from the certainty of death. Loss of siblings or close friends pierces your illusions of immortality ---- and that there will always be a tomorrow. Loss of a spouse or longtime companion signals the end of a whole era of being a "we", and leaves you alone to laugh and cry at the highs and lows of life. Loss of a child is the unthinkable, and in my mind, the ultimate loss. It is sad enough when children must bury their parents. But it is horrible beyond imagination when parents must bury their children ---- the tragic by-product of wars, famine, violence, accidents, and illnesses without cures.

Unfinished Business

Cleaning out a storage closet a few years ago, I discovered hidden under a pile of towels a little white baby blanket that my older sister had given me when our second daughter was born. It had been and was still so special to me. I hadn't seen the blanket for so long that I feared it was lost. But now I'd found it at long last.

Before she gave me the blanket, my sister had lent me several items, always expecting me to return them. The blanket was different. She had used it for each of her three daughters, all older than my children. Then she had given it to me to keep. My sister was generous with her friends but had rarely been with me. In turn I remained somewhat distant from her to avoid being hurt. We had a history of never fully trusting each other.

After many months of being out of touch with her, I learned that she was gravely ill and went to visit her. As we talked openly, I mentioned how much I treasured the little blanket. For that moment, we felt extremely close. We made plans for the future, including a picnic at Moss Beach once she was well, a place where long before we had shared a happy afternoon. At some level, however, both of us knew that these plans were a fantasy. Not only would she not recover, but even if she did, we never would be able to sustain these brief moments of shared vulnerability.

She died the next day.

The little blanket is still in the family. I always feel sad when I open a drawer of the cabinet and come across that symbol of a shaky continuity between us, a reminder of the relationship that was never truly solid. And Lionel Richie's line, "Wherever you are, I hope someone's taking care of you," chokes me up.

Deaths like my sister's are complex, tinged with bittersweet feelings. They involve the loss of relationships that didn't completely jell, full of good intentions and well-defended boundaries. Their language is predictable, rehearsed, drained of feelings ---- made up mostly of empty conversations at family get-togethers and holiday and birthday cards with brief impersonal messages.

Pure Sadness

Other deaths are purer and even more painful losses, for we have no mixed feelings. We have loved and been loved deeply ---- no one has held back anything. There are no regrets, only a profound sense of loss, and sadness that our time together couldn't go on indefinitely.

It is spring of 1966. We are making Christmas cookies. The irony of baking holiday cookies in April would have delighted my grandmother. But she can't enjoy it. She died last week. And for her memorial, I decide that baking the Christmas cookies she so loved is perfect for the occasion. As I laugh and cry, I wish she were here to laugh and cry with me. What a void her absence has left in my life.

Ever since my grandmothers's death, each Christmas I take out the list of cookie recipes written in her now faded handwriting. Many holiday seasons I crazily rushed to bake all twelve of the recipes, exhausted by Christmas Eve. Then one year I realized memories of my grandmother were hidden beneath my franticness.

When I slowed down, making only a few kinds of cookies, those fond memories of my grandmother flooded my mind. I remembered endless games of gin rummy, all waged in heated battle, and hands of solitaire so frustrating that we took turns cheating to finally win! I loved recalling all our cooking adventures, including a whole afternoon spent baking nine layers of a quite elegant French cake, only to ruin our masterpiece by caramelizing the frosting completely into solid "rock" so hard we couldn't cut the cake. We laughed until tears rolled down our cheeks about the literal truth of the saying, "You can't have your cake and eat it too!" I couldn't leave out our outings in downtown San Francisco where I was dressed to the nines, wearing gloves and a dress (not my favorite jeans). I didn't even chew gum and had a wonderful time anyway. Most of all, I recalled that she was never too busy to teach me to knit or to listen to whatever I had to say.

It's Only a Story

Death in a movie or a book, though not directly affecting your life, can cut deeply into old wounds.

For several weeks I had been reading Wilson Rawl's *Where the Red Fern Grows* to Francesca, my then ten-year-old daughter. The story, a fictionalized autobiography of the author's own childhood, tells of a boy's many happy adventures with two dogs, his constant companions. Later, one dog is gored by a mountain lion and dies, followed by the death of his sister dog. The story is so realistic, I hurt with the boy. I'm reminded of the death of my own dog Duke when I was twelve. Then I recall the death of my grandfather when I was three and all the other painful losses of loved ones and I break down sobbing.

My daughter tries to comfort me saying, "It's only a story, Mom." For a moment, though, I am inconsolable.

Before His Time

A man I knew suffered an early tragic loss. He was three-and-a-half years old when his mother died in a freak car accident. Though with her at the time, miraculously he was unharmed ---- physically.

His father was overcome by grief and unable to use his bond with his son to comfort them both. Instead the father became distant and withdrew into his work. He and his son each remained alone, not able to share their sorrow.

Within a year, the boy's father remarried. This change somewhat lifted the father's depression but only deepened the boy's. For the new mother, though kind, was self-centered and emotionally limited, unable to help the boy ease his suffering. She chose to make only minimum mention of his mother's death, so it slipped out of sight.

Sensing what he had to do, the boy decided to put on a happy face ---- to act as if everything was all right; no one need worry about him. Known as a carefree child with a quick sense of humor, he was always a delight to be around. As he grew older, he became the life of every party, able to put on a good show at the drop of a hat.

It's probably no surprise that he became a movie actor, and a very good one at that, gaining a faithful following. In his late twenties he moved abroad to Italy, married, and settled in Rome. To anyone who didn't know him well, he seemed to have it all. Professionally he was a great success ---- and he never lacked for friends.

Publicly he continued to put on a good show, but as the years passed, he was less and less able to cover over his pain. Those close to him could see the increased tension in his marriage, the squabbling between him and his wife, and the ever greater quantities of alcohol he consumed. And when he wasn't medicated by alcohol or high on the challenge of the moment, all of his sadness began to penetrate his carefree veneer.

Time went on. One wife left; he found another. The new one had been attracted to him largely for his money and glamour and somewhat resembled his second mother in her emotional limitations. In spite of her weaknesses, his fear of being alone kept him tied to her. His drinking escalated as did his inner pain, no longer concealed by the happy mask he had worn.

And one dark night, after a succession of many failed suicide attempts, he slit his throat and ended it all. Shortly before his death, he told a friend that he felt he was "playing to an ever diminishing audience" and he couldn't go on with the show any longer.

I still miss him.

He was my brother.

* * *

What do you do when a loved one dies? You cry. You cry a lot. You take time alone to cry. You cry on nice friends' shoulders and nice friends sometimes cry with you. You take refuge in short-term goals and just getting through each day. When something or someone reminds you of the person ---- events you shared, anniversaries, the person's birthday, holidays ---- you cry. Buckets of tears are necessary. You let yourself remember, and you cry for what you no longer have together. You trust that time will ease your pain, and thank goodness, eventually it does.

When there is unfinished business with the person who dies ---- old resentments, unexpressed love, unfulfilled expectations ---- a final goodbye may be thwarted by bottled-up guilt and anger. All of this can and needs to be worked through ---- in writing, talking to friends, or some symbolic communication ---- so that you can let go and live on.

* * *

Perhaps, somewhere in heaven our loved ones live on, having a grand old party together, waiting for us to join them. Perhaps...but in this life, losing someone special just hurts...a lot.

Another Brief Intermission

Life is too important to take seriously.
                    ---- Anonymous

The previous five chapters have been full of heavy issues. Unfortunately, they are part of life. If at any point such negative factors start to overwhelm you, and junking it all and moving to the Bahamas is not a viable option, try to find readily available resources to keep you centered. May I suggest the following activities?

- Feeding ducks in the park, who, unlike you, are unaware of the state of the world
- Listening to a melodic phrase of an opera, a symphony, or some other powerful music that touches you deeply
- Reading an eloquent passage from a book that expresses eternal truths
- Seeing a distracting or escapist movie
- Taking a stroll through an aquarium, museum or zoo
- Visiting a cemetery
- Doing something for someone less fortunate than you

- Slowly drinking a cup of rich Italian coffee
- Meditating in an empty church
- Savoring a lazy couple of hours in idle talk with a friend
- Caring for a well-loved baby or child for an afternoon
- Watching the ocean waves crashing as they have since before you were born and will continue to do so long after you are gone (if you live near a coast, that is)
- *Not* reading the headlines or watching the evening news for a couple of days

And if the world feels too dark and dreary, seek professional guidance. Blocked tears and anger can lead to depression. A good therapist can help you sort out your feelings and explore different choices.

When I begin to feel caught in a daily treadmill beyond my control or depressed about the bad and sad things in life, I like to return to nature. In a beautiful natural setting I gaze at majestic mountains, tall trees, sunsets and stars, the flickering campfire, scurrying squirrels. Dipping into nature helps me strip life down to its essentials and focus on what is important ---- enjoying each day and spending time with those I love.

* * *

It is a new year, a chance for a fresh start, an opportunity for order and sensible living I don't want to miss. Like many others forever involved in what I feel are 'big' projects, I have difficulty with what feels to me like the mundane ---- paperwork, dishes, dusting, doctor appointments, dental appointments, phone calls, more paperwork.

I have already searched in five different stationery stores for just the right calendar ---- one to give an overview of the month, lines for the hours of each day, spaces on the side for phone numbers and occasional notes ---- a calendar big enough to hold legible writing yet little enough to fit on the table beside my office chair.

I go to three more stores picking up and opening an endless variety of calendars. None of them are quite right. I want something to give order to my days, peace to my mind, and answers to my life. Perhaps the stationery store is not the place to make it all come together.

What a pity that life's dilemmas can't be solved so easily.

PART III. UTILIZE THE POSSIBILITY OF WHAT CAN BE:

You Can Never Have Too Many Mangos

If you asked me what I came in this world to do,
I will tell you:
I came to live out loud.
----Emile Zola

Though we have no choice about our origins and little control over the forces of humankind and world at large, there are many ways to live our lives and spend our time. Some may be financially or in other ways productive; some are more or less satisfying and enjoyable; some involve fellow human beings at varying levels of closeness. My basic theory is this: Just as in family life, when we're expected to clean up our own rooms and make a dent in the general household clutter, we need to take responsibility for our own lives and the clutter of the world.

Part III explores various options in life available to everyone:

- How to give meaning to your days ---- deal with the *have-to's* and *want-to's* and weed out unnecessary *should's*;

- My version of grabbing an unexpected opportunity that came my way;
- The kind of support systems possible;
- The *why's, how's,* and *if's* of choosing a traveling companion to accompany you on your life journey;
- The agony and ecstasy of raising children —— for those who care to embark on this particular adventure;
- The reality that you can remember the past and plan for the future, but all you have is today;
- How to keep a perspective on this fact: Although everything matters, it is also true that nothing matters.

On a morning walk, I pass by the corner fruit and vegetable store offering a "special" on mangos, four for a dollar. I buy twelve. "Why so many?" asks my husband. "You can never have too many mangos," I reply. And the truth of the matter is this: Whenever I have brought home mangos, including ones well past their prime, they're always gobbled up. I've never thrown one out.

Mangos symbolize what spices up life, not a necessity but an always welcome delicacy. They're exotic and bring to mind meandering through crowded marketplaces in small towns of Mexico or lying on clean, fine-sand beaches of Hawaii. Mangos speak of relaxation, vacation, *"la dolce vita."* *"Muy mango"* in Spanish means "cool," "the way to be," "the way to live." Even when mangos come with outrageous price tags, from time to time I love to eat one. Picks up the day. Gives it a bit of enjoyable decadence.

I don't want to have too many days without mangos.

TEN

Each Day Is A Blank Canvas

Does this path have a heart?
If it does, the path is good; if it doesn't, it is of no use.
Both paths lead nowhere; but one has a heart, the other doesn't.
---- Carlos Castaneda, from
The Teachings of Don Juan

You can measure public success or failure by the size of your house or car or how impressed other people are with your job. But these measures don't gauge the quality of your life or whether you are enjoying it. You'll receive no As or Fs to show you're on track or off in left field. And unlike in the movies, there's no music to tell you all is well or to signal you're spinning your wheels in "quiet desperation."

So where will you put your energy and how will you occupy your days?

Warding off the *should's* to keep from being smothered gives many people trouble: I should work harder. I should exercise more. I should not leave this relationship. I should stay with this job. I should watch less television. Examine these *should's* carefully, and separate them from your *have-to's* and *want-to's*.

Have-To's

The *have-to's* are part of survival, ideally related to a lifestyle you choose. They may include earning a minimum salary each month to keep a roof over your head, attaining certain grades in school to qualify for a special training program, doing particular chores so you don't suffocate in dust or dirty clothes, or finishing tasks required for an assignment at work. Unless independent wealth provides you with the luxury of paying others to do the *have-to's*, you must address them or they will forever tap on your shoulder and spoil your fun.

You may be able to find meaning and self-fulfillment doing many of these *have-to's*, from a novel way to earn a living to deriving pleasure from cooking a top-notch meal. At all times, though, distinguish between a *have-to* to attain *your* goals and a *should* to please or appease others (such as continuing to live in a place or work in a job that doesn't make you happy).

No lifestyle is the *correct* lifestyle. No line of work is more important than any other. Advanced training in school or in the outside world doesn't make you better than anyone else, though it can expose you to new ideas and offer job opportunities.

When a particular fifty-six-year-old woman called for an appointment, I had second and third thoughts. Even in the first brief telephone conversation it was evident that she directed venom and blame toward her eighty-year-old, well-to-do mother, upon whom she was financially dependent: "It's her fault that my life is so miserable. Picking up the tab for my therapy and for everything else is the *least* she can do." I choked back an urge to rebuke her immaturity then and there. Instead, I told her I couldn't be of help.

Regardless how much money such a person is willing to pay, I can choose whether to accept her as a patient. Others might feel different, but I don't care to put my time and energy into somebody's irresponsible wallowing.

Of course, it's never too late even to switch lines of work altogether ---- with obvious exceptions, such as suddenly becoming a middle-aged Olympic gymnast or late-blooming musical child prodigy ---- though shifting gears may make waves and puzzle loved ones. Even if you need N number of years to prepare for your new venture, one way or another, you'll be N number of years older anyway. So take a chance and persevere. What's there to lose?

Emily, one of my colleagues, left a prestigious, demanding job after her second child was born, a job that made her father proud but one she'd grown to hate. Because she wasn't ambitious and had always wanted to stay home, she was overjoyed to have the opportunity to immerse herself in cooking and to participate in activities with her children. After a year, however, she realized that she had underestimated how much she needed more stimulation when the high point of her day was clipping coupons and figuring out which store gave the best price on cheese. Not that there's anything wrong with wanting to get a good deal. But given Emily's emotional makeup, decisions like these didn't challenge her enough. So Emily went on to train for a lower-pressure career. She worked three afternoons a week and didn't feel so stretched. This choice provided a happy balance to her life.

Talking with a forest ranger at one of our favorite campsites, I complimented him on how beautifully the area was maintained. He responded by telling me that for years he had earned a good living as an accountant but finally decided that city life wasn't for him. So he went back to school to study forestry, and for more than twenty years, he and his wife had lived in the woods. "I consider the whole park to be my own private garden, and I love to take good care of it," he said contentedly. What a joy to meet people who take pride in their work and do it well.

Want-To's

These involve spending free time in enjoyable ways. *Want-to's* can range from deciding what kinds of music, food, or art you like or dislike to assessing which friends and pastimes restore or drain your energy. Charles Schulz, the creator of the Peanuts cartoon, when asked why he didn't retire, answered, "I could sit around all day and watch 'Jeopardy' with my dog, but he never knows any of the answers." The key is to spend as much time as possible in satisfying activities with kindred spirits (and as little as possible in uninteresting activities with people who bore or offend you).

A woman called my radio talk show to tell me that her family had asked what she would like for Mother's Day. After some thought she replied, "I'd like to go to the park with all of you and play softball, only this time I get to be at bat as long as I want." She said her family followed through with flying colors. Other than a small stint in the field, she remained at bat for a couple of hours, experiencing a magnificent, memorable Mother's Day. Though her wish was granted on one special day, life can be a chain of special days, each filled with endless possibilities.

In *The Second Coming*, Walker Percy stated, "Not once had he been present for his life. So his life had passed like a dream. Is it possible for people to miss their lives in the same way one misses a plane? And how is it that death, the nearness of death, can restore a missed life?" Life is too short. Don't put off what you want to do until "someday" which may not come.

Should's

The remaining *should's* ---- seductive and dangerous companions ---- can lock you into a prison. They may take the form of lame excuses for staying in unhappy work or in personal situations out of habit or duty, your need for security, or your fear of what others will say.

Looking quite "down," Ed consulted me for advice. Although his life in general was "not bad," his high-paying executive job was boring and rather unchallenging, there was friction in his marriage, and he was unhappy. He loved fishing, skiing, and camping, but hadn't fished or skied for years, largely because his wife June hated these sports.

Married ten years without children, Ed and June constantly bickered and felt little joy. The more Ed talked, the more evident it became to me how completely mismatched they were and how burnt out he was at work. But he was adamantly against making any major life changes, in part because he feared his parents' disapproval.

A short stint of therapy helped Ed to eventually resume the outdoor activities that he loved so and to communicate more openly with June, though sadly she wanted no part of therapy. Most tragic, however ---- Ed's "not bad" existence was "not good" ---- yet he would never have another life to live.

Staying with *should's* allows you the illusion of fulfillment, but actually detours and distracts you from being aware of the brevity of life. Beware of these *should's*. They are useless leftovers from being an obedient child, and they belong in the trash can. If they dominate your life, you need to lay the ghosts from the past more completely to rest.

* * *

Editing to meet a deadline for the first edition of my book *Getting Off the Merry-Go-Round: You Can Live without Compulsive Habits* involved several days of long hours at the word processor, the help of my computer-savvy husband, and the patience of our not-always-patient children. When I wrapped up the project and got it ready to send off to the publisher, I found myself stepping back and wondering whether the whole thing was ridiculous. Wanting to convey important thoughts, I had written the manuscript carefully and comprehensively. But bookstore shelves are lined with books, even many excellent ones. Isn't it foolish to spend so much time and energy on yet another one? When I expressed these thoughts to my husband, he piped in: "What else are you going to do with your time?" True.

You can bury your days in the upkeep of life punctuated by escapes into television, food, drink, shopping and other distractions. Unless you are passionately involved in something meaningful, however, all your activity is hollow.

So onward I plodded. Months later a much-welcomed package arrived ---- the book, finally in print ---- earlier than I expected. It was hard to believe; even I was impressed. It looked fantastic, beyond what I had imagined. As much as I had labored over each word, seeing them all come together somehow in a real honest-to-goodness printed book was most exciting.

And to add to the magnificence of the day, within hours after the book arrived a phone call came from the publicist assigned to set up my book tour. Wonderful. It will be just like I imagined: "Unknown author writes runaway best-seller, bounces from one national talk show to the next, and helps millions." Sounded great. I even selected a title for the movie version of the book, *Compulsive Days and Sleepless Nights,* and wondered if Martin Sheen would agree to play the lead.

In the next few weeks, however, reality set in. Rather than the full-fledged national tour I had in mind, I went to only three West Coast cities.

Though at first I took it personally, I was told that getting high-powered publicity for well-written or poorly written books by first-time unknown authors is rare. Rather, only in high prestige publishing houses do books by or about famous celebrities, especially ones with sordid tales to tell, receive the time and money, despite the quality of the writing. And although the third chapter of my book details a seemingly seamy codependent relationship between our two cats, Michelangelo and Sasha, no famous celebrity is involved. So since my name is not a household word, I got busy doing the publicity myself ---- tough stuff for a Type-A personality desperately trying to learn the art of delegating responsibility to others.

Gradually I became more and more involved. Frantically I phoned national television producers around the country, some whose shows like "Oprah" and "Donahue" I had appeared on before. I played telephone tag ad nauseam with people who didn't return phone calls. And I tried without success to collect favors from national and local showbiz people who "owed me one," individuals for whom I had dropped everything in the past. Most of them couldn't remember my name. I started to feel ragged and disjointed.

From what I heard in author circles, being on with Oprah, Donahue, Geraldo, Sally Jessie Rafael, Ted Koppel, and so on, would supposedly pave my way to success ---- possibly having my book rank among greats with the likes of M. Scott Peck and Eric Erickson, not to mention Tolstoy and the Bible. Well-meaning loved ones and newly self-appointed mentors fueled my quest: "The national exposure could make the difference. You have got to do your full publicity thrust in the first three months, or your book will vanish from the shelves, never to be seen again." Horrors, I thought. I worked too hard for that to happen. I had to make more phone calls. Surely the next one would make the difference.

I had to persist. It wouldn't last forever. The *could-be's* and *should-be's* clobbered me on the head.

Life felt hectic. Each day was an obstacle course of family and professional responsibilities: trying to phone yet another television producer ---- at best one phone call was returned for every five I made; luncheons with my new entourage of supportive publicity consultants intent on beating the system; and rewriting for the "nth" time the perfect letter which would entice some producer to squeeze me on a national show because I would be the "just right" consultant.

Meanwhile, I had given away to a variety of folks almost all of the two hundred books I ordered ---- journalists who had interviewed me in the past and other possible sources of publicity, patients, new friends, old friends, relatives who couldn't "just say no," acquaintances at places of business, friends and teachers of my children. And I have to admit that each time I gave a book away or heard some nice remark about how the book had truly made a difference and helped someone, I temporarily felt a tremendous surge of joy and remembered why I wrote the book in the first place. But dreams of glory didn't prevent me from realizing that I best not give up my day job.

My sanity began to feel bombarded and sidetracked by my latent ambition. I thought I was in control of the whole situation, but at some point I began to lose it. I often skipped breakfast and forgot about lunch ---- I who had been a compulsive eater. I slept fitfully at night and had nightmares about getting on important television shows but becoming lost on the way to the airport and about my house being full of animals slowly starving to death. Each morning I woke up with lists in my mind of all the people I should phone and write the next day.

Fortunately, an important perspective came from John Carmen's column in the *San Francisco Chronicle*. He listed stories that various television talk shows were using to raise their ratings during the sweeps:

An Oprah Winfrey sample: "Dad and I Date the Same Women." Promo for an Empty Nest episode: "Carol loses her lover in the Bermuda Triangle." Geraldo Rivera presented the "Battle of the Best Bodies," pitting Chippendale dancers against Penthouse Pets in aerobic exercises. Phil Donahue investigated transvestite prostitutes and sisters who swap husbands.

As I recounted these subjects to a friend, I jokingly said, "I have finally figured out how to get on these shows. I will divorce my husband, Virg, who will have a sex change and become Virginia, and I will have a sex change and become Carl. We will remarry and adopt a bisexual dog who will have relations with both our male and female cats. Then I will send off letters to major shows suggesting that I be both example and consultant, demonstrating unusual family constellations." When I told this story to my daughter, Michelle, she felt my chances of getting on shows would increase if I had my sex change during the program and I wore sequins.

These fantasies were starting to be fun. Then it dawned on me that I had not been having fun for a number of weeks. A meaningful project had become derailed by a series of *should's*. Instead of basking in the joy of having my book available to help those who might benefit from it, somewhere in the transition from writer to author, I allowed life to become drudgery, and I lost "me."

* * *

No matter who you are or what you do, every day is a blank canvas to paint your life on ---- with subdued tones, conservative and safe, and little exploration of the unknown or with vibrant colors in untried experimental combinations.

There is no right way that you should paint your canvas, however, for no one but you can know what feels good.

Sometimes a creative enterprise comes together and works, perhaps with only a few corrective touches. At other times, it simply doesn't work: You step back, consider the project an interesting learning experience, throw it out, and wash your brushes for the next one. But you only have a limited number of canvases to paint on. Don't waste them.

ELEVEN

When Opportunity Knocks, Ready Or Not, Open The Door

Four things come not back ---- the spoken word, the sped arrow,
the past life, the neglected opportunity.
---- Arabian proverb

Opportunities appear at strange times and in unanticipated disguises, often when you are unprepared or busy with other projects.

A friend arrives in town unexpectedly and wants to see you; you're in the middle of meeting a deadline. The love of your life calls to suggest a dinner date ---- just as you finish eating. At the last minute free symphony tickets are offered; you had planned to go to bed early. A course you've always wanted to take is being offered at a nearby college on Wednesdays, but this is the night for your regular card game. You win a vacation trip to Hawaii for two, but there is no one special in your life to travel with just now.

Or perhaps an unusual part-time job comes out of the blue and beckons your career in a new direction...

* * *

March 1980. An unexpected phone call comes from a man I've never met regarding a subject I know almost nothing about: Would I be interested in hosting a regular three-hour, five-morning-a-week call-in talk show? asks the program director of San Francisco radio station KSFO.

I'm speechless. Coming from a family with an outgoing older sister and an older brother who had been a movie actor, I always considered myself to be the shy, reserved one. Furthermore, since finishing my psychiatric residency, I have worked only part-time for nine years. I'm used to doing some consulting and spending not more than five to seven hours a week with patients. The youngest of my four children is barely two years old, and I have strong feelings about trying to be the mother I never had. To make the call even more incongruous, I have only rarely heard talk radio and am not exactly sure what a call-in show host does.

Biding time while I catch my balance, I ask for more information. I learn that it is not because of my reputation (good or bad) that KSFO has phoned me. It seems a Los Angeles psychologist, Toni Grant, has markedly upped her station's audience share. Hence, in the minds of media management, "Lady shrinks raise ratings." KSFO sorely needs a boost since the recent departure of a host whose show had dominated the market with unheard of high ratings ("fifteen share," as they say in the biz). It turns out the program director has never heard of me; he simply found the name of this "lady shrink" in the small print of the Yellow Pages! Thank you, "Ma Bell."

Though being on the radio sounds far-fetched, I'm intrigued. I tell the KSFO man I'll think it over. In the next few days, I have an ongoing dialogue with myself. Do I want to do this?

On the one hand, there is my professional orientation. I come from a six-and-a-half year, five-day-a-week analysis at

Hanna Pavilion in Cleveland, Ohio ---- so "classic" that I even had to pay for days I missed for my grandmother's funeral. That experience was followed by an equally classic psychiatry residency at San Francisco's Mt. Zion Hospital, where residents kept an analytic stance and tried in every way to stay "neutral and nondirective." If I go on the radio, the real "me" ---- a very fallible human being ---- will surely show through.

On the other hand, I've always been a risk taker, enjoying ventures into new territory ---- especially outrageous ones that can make for good storytelling to friends or family afterward. The words of a consultant during a residency echo in my mind: " You'll be yourself in twenty years, so you might as well do so now."

So, why not go for it?

I call the KSFO program director back. Too late. They've already picked a psychologist who will start April 1. I try to shelve the whole issue but end up thinking about it a great deal. I tune in April 1 to hear this "other" woman. After listening to her, my mind starts to race. What an opportunity to educate people, to do preventive psychiatry, to reach thousands who would otherwise never get near a psychiatrist's office!

A neighbor is director of public relations at KNBR, another San Francisco station. With her help I do a number of public affairs tapes that air at odd hours of the day and night. (Seventeen-year-old Andrea is most surprised to catch me at six one morning ---- there's no hiding place from Mom. Mario, age two, asks, "How did Mommy get in the little black box?")

I then make a "demo tape" for the KSFO program director and inquire about being a fill-in for the psychologist. "Compared to her," I tell him, "I have far better training and far more life experience." "You actually told him that?" asks my husband.

June 1980. My chutzpah pays dividends. I'm covering during the one-week vacation of the psychologist on the morning show. Having never done live radio before, I feel like I'm in hard labor in the delivery room on Monday at 9:00 A.M. The baby's head has already appeared, and there's no turning back.

One of the first calls comes from a troubled woman named Theresa. I barely restrain myself from mentioning that Theresa is also the name of my seven-year-old daughter's pet rabbit. Though nervous, I'm still conscious of exceedingly poor taste.

By Friday I am more confident. Not only am I in my element, but I've learned that I have access to the large music library at KSFO. My on-air subject for the day is "If you had your life to live over, what would you change?". I pick out ten favorite songs starting with "Those Were the Days My Friend," ("We thought they'd never end,") moving into "Time Goes By," ("You must remember this..."). After a few tunes, I'm jolted out of my bliss by a reminder from the newsman that this is supposed to be a *call-in* show; I should take calls and not just play music. A friend later tells me that I'm obviously a "closet D. J."

The week has gone well. I'm having a ball. I've gotten positive feedback from other talk-show hosts and employees at KSFO and from many callers. In addition, during this time I do my first television consultation ---- a live interview about the "Trailside Killer" on the five o'clock news. I'm overwhelmed being in the spotlight, fascinated by the show-biz quality of television (including the quantity of pancake makeup on the news anchor's face), and [in 1980] aware of not being very knowledgeable about serial, mass, or any other kinds of killers. When asked about the profile of such a killer, I truthfully answer, "I'm not sure." Later, friends tell me how impressed they were. Not only did they like what I was wearing, but I was so secure that even though I was an expert, I didn't have to put on pretensions about knowing everything.

Clearly I'm on my way.

* * *

Spring 1981. Most of a year has passed, and my media "career" is far from launched. My "demo tape" is making the rounds with a "Media Resume" (truthful but jazzed up and minus the stuffy academic details). My efforts lead to several guest spots on radio stations around the Bay Area ---- KNBR, KJAZ, KTIM and KLOK ---- and a twelve-part series, "You and Your Child," for KALW, the San Francisco educational station. A number of times I also fill in at KGO for the regular morning and afternoon talk-show hosts and the "then" KGO psychologist. An all-night slot gives me a chance to play Cat Stevens' "Morning Has Broken" at dawn to thousands up and down the West Coast. What a thrill!

People at KGO are most kind to me. The assistant program director is encouraging, talk-show hosts give me pointers, a veteran newscaster takes me under his wing and coaches me about what to do and what not to do on the air. But in spite of all this support, I don't get my own show for several months.

December 1981. At last! I am finally given my own show ---- Saturday afternoons, eventually moving to evenings.

April 1990. For almost ten years now, I've had my own show.

5:30 P.M. Today, it goes something like this... I leave for KGO, accompanied by Mario ---- now twelve and no longer wondering how Mom got inside the little black box. While I am on the air he will play with Phillip, the engineer's son.

6:00 P.M. My mail box at the station is stuffed with several books, a few notes of appreciation, follow-up reports from past callers, a pamphlet about grieving from Sister Marian at a local hospital, who often sends me helpful material, and a postcard from Hawaii from a former San Francisco woman who called me a year ago. (She had felt stuck in a dead-end job, and when I asked her what she really wanted to do, she answered, "To live in Hawaii.") The postcard simply says, "Thanks for listening and giving me a push."

In the minutes before I'm on the air, I say "Hello" to the newsman, the engineer, and the producer who screens the calls, look over commercials, and try to get organized. Most of all, I shift gears from normal life to being "up" for the show.

7:00 P.M. I move into the studio, hook up my earphones, lay out a ton of back-up material for emergency use in case the phones should go dead, and mentally get set to go.

I introduce metro traffic and let the opening theme run out. Now it is my turn. I push the "on" button: "Good evening. I'm Dr. Carla Perez, KGO's psychiatrist, with you until 10:00 P.M. We are live. Our Saturday evening together is your chance to call about any area of your life you're stuck in or feel concerned about." I go on a bit about a topic on my mind: unavoidable vs. avoidable pain in life (the latter, the unfinished business from childhood). Then I switch to the first three-minute commercial cluster, one of fifteen that I must squeeze in during the three-hour show. I recall a letter from a woman who wrote, "Dr. Perez, I write down all the commercials that run on your show so that I'm sure to remember them when I go to the store."

Meanwhile my producer is performing magic. He has already received several calls, screened a few inappropriate ones from being aired, given people aliases when they want anonymity, and summarized three callers' questions on the screen in front of me.

Chuck is the first on-air caller. He's worried about his out-of-control spending and debts. "For what?" I ask. "Ice cream, a girlfriend, an expensive car." After a few minutes talking together, I suggest he try Debtor's Anonymous.

Three minutes of local news on the half-hour and then I'm with Ellen. In a slow, sad voice, she launches into an endless story: She married an alcoholic, realized she needed to look out for herself, went back to school, earned an M.B.A., divorced, and retired three years ago. Time is going by, other calls are waiting. I prod Ellen: "How can I help?" She has invested in "junk" bonds, lost a great deal of money, and feels depressed. Now she's crying. As I start to give her support, the clock says I must put her on hold through a commercial cluster. As we talk in greater depth about her fears and anger at those who have let her down, she gradually calms down. I urge her to seek financial advice and go into therapy. And ask her to call me back. More commercials.

David starts out coherently enough, talking about his girlfriend but soon lapses into tangential issues. He's writing to all his girlfriend's friends, his mother's high-school friends, important government officials. After a few more minutes, it becomes apparent that he is psychotic, and I urge him to go to a hospital emergency room or community mental health center for help.

During the commercial breaks, I often converse with the newsman who updates me on his latest girlfriends. Newsbreaks give me the chance to hear what the producer has been doing during the week. The engineer and I discuss the latest trials and tribulations of our respective teenage daughters.

I feel immensely appreciative to have an engineer. Last summer for a number of weeks, I did my show *a cappella*, which meant doing my own engineering. Though I made no major errors and in fact felt rather proud to be carrying the whole thing off solo, I was so focused on remembering not to drink liquids (no time to go to the bathroom), getting all the commercial cartridges in the right spots, and catching the network news on the exact second, I could barely concentrate on the callers.

Steve calls, reminds me that he had called five months ago, desperate and depressed at having relapsed into cocaine, and thanks me for shaking him up and pushing him to get back into Twelve-Step programs. He also mentions how much it meant to him that other callers cared about his welfare.

Because Janet and her husband are separating, she asks what she should tell their three-year-old daughter, Sarah. I suggest Janet make a simple-language book for Sarah, highlighting that Daddy and Mommy have trouble getting along and have decided to live apart, that it is not Sarah's fault, and that Daddy and Mommy will never divorce her.

Gordon calls in wondering about his girlfriend's prescription for Xanax. In fact, several calls relate to the addictive qualities of this drug, a subject I touch on often. I warn people to avoid long-term use of Xanax, Valium, Librium, and other Benzodiazapines. I also advise callers to get a second opinion if their doctors keep prescribing them, the dangers of stopping suddenly, and where to get help to wean themselves from these drugs.

John is concerned about his sister who lives in New York. One day she made small talk with a man at a bus stop. He subsequently followed her, got her phone number, and keeps making threats to harm her if she doesn't go out with him. We discuss the "fatal attraction" phenomenon, maybe seeking a restraining order, and, if necessary for her safety, the possibility she might temporarily move west to stay with her brother.

Ginny, my last caller, asks what to do when her boyfriend orchestrates her life, especially everything she eats; no matter what she says to him, he won't "bug out." I have no time to explore whether she has had similar relationships in the past and possible childhood roots of her present predicament. Nevertheless, this particular relationship sounds so unhealthy I urge Ginny to get out of it.

Time has run out. I sign off the air, Mario signs off with Phillip, and we drive home talking about this and that and munching on the leftovers of snacks he has squeezed out of the vending machines.

What would Freud say if questioned about taking psychiatry to the airwaves? "Why do you ask?"

* * *

January 1993. The KGO program director phones me: "Could you please come into my office? No rush. Whenever you can make it this week." Perhaps he's going to ask me to fill in on week nights? Perhaps he'll give me my long-overdue raise? A few days later, I'm sitting in his office. After several minutes of pleasantries, he says, "Thanks for helping the newsman who was drunk on the air last week. And incidentally, [so-and-so] will be taking over your show this weekend."

I'm dumbfounded. Have I dozed off in the middle of his sentence and missed something? I mumble meaningless words and stumble out of the room. He later tells others "how well Carla received the news." In the following days, fellow talk-show hosts are most kind and supportive. They tell me shocking tales about the first times they were fired and how they eventually accepted firings as a regular part of radio life.

KGO is apparently having an "intellectual cleansing," and the story makes the *San Francisco Chronicle*. Columnist Herb Caen writes, "The program director not only has fired a college professor as a talk-show host, he dumped a psychoanalyst and a state senator as well." [Like most people, Herb hasn't sorted out the confusing labels of "psychiatrist" (M. D.), "psychologist" (Ph.D. or Psy.D.), and "psychoanalyst" (advanced specialty)]. With one stroke of the pen, Herb Caen has given me three additional years of specialty training and turned me into a prestigious "psychoanalyst." (Oh well, we're all "shrinks," and without clothes, we're all naked.)

* * *

The point of my "radio days" story is simply this: If an intriguing opportunity opens up to you, grab it. Unless there is a good reason to say "no", say "yes". Some ventures will work out well and others will end up being memorable learning experiences. Such is life. Recall the proverb that introduced this chapter: "Four things come not back ― the spoken word, the sped arrow, the past life, the neglected opportunity."

TWELVE

Choose Your Support System Carefully

A friend is one...before whom I may think aloud.
---- Ralph Waldo Emerson

R elationships with others enrich our existence and provide sounding boards from which our own lives can resonate. As we wing our way from day to day, it's comforting to share tales of adventures and misadventures with fellow humans.

From casual to intimate, your human support system might be composed of several types of acquaintances and friends:

- Brief encounters of the positive kind
- Community contacts
- Personal service network
- Long-term friends from "way back"
- Activity friends
- Good family members
- Always there, foul-weather friends
- Close-to-the-heart friends

Brief Encounters of the Positive Kind

A brief encounter with someone you've never met before and probably will never see again happens by chance and may last from a few minutes to a few weeks or more.

Almost every day, you stand next to people at the bus stop, in the grocery store, or in the movie line. Or you meet the refrigerator repair person or the electric meter reader. You might spend a few hours with someone who rides next to you on a train or airplane.

During this shared time you might make no contact, or you might reach out ---- with anything from idle chatter about today's news to a bolder move toward getting to know each other better. Many of us have fun with encounters like these when we're on vacation or on foreign soil but neglect to make use of comparable opportunities on our home turf.

One evening, the day before our family was to go on vacation, our washing machine broke down. With a lot of cajoling, pleading, and begging, repairman Ralph agreed to make a last-minute evening house call. He quickly fixed the machine and to our surprise, did not overcharge us. We were feeling extremely grateful and offered him beer and snacks. He not only proved to be a decent person but quite a raconteur as well.

With graphic language and comic details, Ralph told a story about his family. Several weeks earlier, his daughter's boyfriend had begun to make himself more and more at home in Ralph's house ---- staying longer and later, eating greater quantities of his food, and finally cleaning out his beer supply. For Ralph, the beer was the last straw. He took his daughter aside and instructed her, in no uncertain terms, to make it clear to her boyfriend that he should "stay the hell out of her old man's liquor cabinet."

Our appliance breakdown became a memorable one-time encounter full of "can-you-top-this?" stories and much laughter with a delightful man!

Community Contacts

Though only bit parts in your total life drama, short exchanges with merchants in all walks of your life ---- at the gas station, pizza parlor, shoe repair store, or pharmacy can be enjoyable, too. Not just pleasant additions to your day, these encounters can define your own special town within a larger community. Obviously the longer you live in one neighborhood, the greater the continuity of these relationships. Over the years, you might discuss everything from the weather to local and world events to the triumphs of and concerns about your children.

Years ago we used to rent videos from a store filled with a wide range of foreign films. But we were never comfortable there. The woman who owned the store and the employees who mimicked her demeanor were arrogant and rude. A nearby bookstore, although convenient, employed similar personnel. I always left both stores in a bad mood. Offensive shopowners and salespeople can be like irritating splinters. After several months I realized that feeling emotionally battered by these encounters was unnecessary. Why put up with guaranteed unpleasantness? Who needs it? Instead I discovered other video and bookstores with good vibrations. I leave them with a smile.

In many areas of life you have little or no choice. Unless you live in a very small town, however, the sky is the limit as to which shops and restaurants you patronize.

Personal Service Network

This network represents those individuals who regularly provide personal service for you and your family ---- doctors, dentists, accountants. Depending on your lifestyle, you might add to the list your own hairdresser, manicurist, masseuse, chiropractor, and therapist, too. Although our family has had to let go of a few bad eggs, over the years we have found professionals who are not only technically competent in their fields but ---- equally important ---- emotionally caring. This mix of skill and care takes the sting out of what otherwise can be physically and/or financially painful experiences. Granted, if you need brain surgery, you want only competence; it matters little whether the doctor is cordial or even has a personality at all. In other personal service areas, however, nice people make your days more enjoyable.

Long-Term Friends from "Way Back"

When possible, keeping in touch with one or more long-term friends from "way back" is a real plus. Of course, maintaining these connections is much easier if you live in the region where you grew up. But with the help of today's communications technology ---- telephone, car phone, cellular phone, fax, e-mail, Internet, overnight express, even old-fashioned letters ---- only some mutual desire to stay in contact is required. Such friends can add an important dimension to your life similar to what happens when you run into a childhood neighbor or attend a high-school reunion. Close in age, both of you have lived through the same period of history together; time has given you comparable scars and wrinkles. You are in the same cycle of your lives and remember the same movies and slang.

You must assess, however, whether you want to hang on to a relationship if it consists of little more than memories from the past. Sometimes, as a high-school friend's mother used to say, the answer to "Should auld acquaintance be forgot?" ought to be a resounding "Yes!"

Activity Friends

With activity friends, you work and complain about the boss, play tennis or poker, or cheer at your children's sports events. Activity friends are the coworkers with whom you share shop talk; fellow parents with whom you swap toddler, teenager, or grandchild tales; volunteers with whom you work on a political campaign or other activity; or classmates with whom you sculpt clay or sweat in aerobics.

You may have intense interactions in particular settings but little contact in other situations. Incidentally, men tend to keep such relationships on a more matter-of-fact level, sharing less personal information, while women are more apt to talk about their intimate concerns. By trial and error, you have to figure out how much closeness or distance feels comfortable for you in a specific relationship.

At one point, my friendliness toward Minette, a good-humored coworker at a hospital where I consulted, led her to expect more from the relationship than suited me. She started to drop in frequently at our home, uninvited, and ask for small personal favors ---- nothing totally unreasonable, but all somewhat irritating. I was in a quandary. I enjoyed my consulting job and interacting with Minette at work, but I was beginning to feel suffocated. Who knows why? Whatever the reason, I was sufficiently annoyed with her intrusiveness into my home life, however, to contemplate quitting.

When I talked about the situation with Emma, an older colleague who worked at the same institution, she mentioned a similar experience with Minette. Emma had to set clear limits about the boundaries in the relationship. Following

Emma's example, I shifted the boundaries of my interaction with Minette from personal to professional only. I was again able to enjoy her as an "activity" friend at work, but not at home.

Good Family Members

As described in the discussion of family relationships in Chapter 3, the bad news is that many of us arrive in adulthood not wanting to stay in close contact with all family members. The good news, however, is that each of us can "adopt" new relatives ---- some officially and others from school, work or other activities. If you marry, for example, you might inherit a few lemons, but you may also hit the jackpot and get some fine "in-laws" out of the deal.

Defying the stereotype, I have lucked out with a wonderful mother-in-law, one of my favorite relatives. We live two hours away from her and visit every month or so, as do the families of her other five children. Usually we bring supplies to try to save her money and extra trips to the stores, but often leave with more goodies than we've brought. She is unbelievably generous ---- apples and pears from her yard; an extra cheese she knows I like; "just a little" money for each of our children; a plant or two or three to remind us of her in our home and to compensate for the green thumb that I don't have; food and drink for the trip back as if we would be on the road for days.

As self-sufficient as she is, we are sad to see her living alone. My father-in-law died many years ago. Sometimes my husband and I speak to her about finding another partner: "How about a look-alike of Ricardo Montalban or Julio Iglesias (her idols)? Or how about Ricardo or Julio himself?" She smiles and then changes the subject. Our visits often hover between tears and laughter.

Always There, Foul-Weather Friends

If you are lucky, over the years you find one or more "always there, foul-weather friends." These are the kind of people who, though you may not have spoken to them for years, at the ring of the phone drop everything to hear the details of your plight. They are there for you when life treats you badly ---- at times of illness, lost jobs, lost relationships, miscarriages, deaths of loved ones, and other catastrophes.

I read a sweet vignette about a little boy who arrived home late from school. When his mother asked what had delayed him, he answered, "My friend's bike broke and I had to help." "But you don't know how to fix a bike," the mother stated. "I had to help him cry," the boy replied.

Foul-weather friends commiserate, offer tissues for your tears, dislike the bad people who have wronged you, and make you feel that you are not intruding in the least, no matter what hour of the day or night. Such "foul-weather friends" sympathize while you wallow, and yet sense just when to give you a push to move on. And somehow you know you're not imposing because you'll be there for them during their times of need, too.

Sometimes a "long-term friend," an "activity friend," or a "good family member" can turn into a "foul-weather friend" when circumstances demand it. Or if you are in a Twelve-Step or other support group, members can comfort you and give you perspective by sharing tales of comparable trials and tribulations. Or, if a crisis is really overwhelming, a warm, insightful therapist may fill this role.

Close-to-the-Heart Friends

Last, but not least, life is greatly enhanced by one or two "close-to-the-heart friends." They might be "long-term friends" or others you have only recently met who happen to be "simpatico" ---- on the same wavelength. You may be at different ages, of different generations, and of the same or opposite sex. What counts is the ease with which you relate to each other, either by words or in comfortable silence. You accept each other's weaknesses and know how not to step on each other's tender spots. Such a friend is like the best of a relationship with a sister or brother without sibling rivalry or any history of teasing or unreturned clothes.

When I speak to people in their seventies, eighties, and nineties who continue to live with zest, they invariably mention how important supportive friends are ---- and the need to continually cultivate new ones, separating the flowers from the weeds.

Visiting with this kind of friend, you feel warmth, you think time passes too quickly, and you can never catch up on everything. You may share a victory, laugh at a disaster, or just quietly pass a pleasant afternoon or evening together. Within reasonable limits, whether you are at your worst or best, you can count on this relationship because you know that it is not fragile. I hope your "close-to-the-heart friends" include your traveling companion in life, if you've found one. But that's a topic for the next chapter.

Ultimately, we each must travel alone. But in our all too impersonal society, a solid support system can take the sting out of aloneness and add immeasurable richness to our lives.

THIRTEEN

A Traveling Companion Can Enhance Your Journey

It doesn't matter what you do in the bedroom as long as you don't do it in the street and frighten the horses.
---- Mrs. Patrick Campbell, English actress

L ove, romance and marriage should be a snap ---- so say the fairy tales. Just kiss the right frog or carry around a glass slipper. Surely Mr. or Ms. Right will materialize, and you'll live happily ever after. It worked for Cinderella, Sleeping Beauty and all the worthy princes. Though we never hear about life in the second chapter ---- how they coped with daily happenings related to money, work, sex, jealousy, dishes, children, friends, relatives, sickness, bad moods, fatigue, aging. . .

Obviously there are no simple answers for establishing a lasting, loving relationship. But I'd like to offer some general guidelines that might help you.

• *First, find yourself and be at peace with your past, so that you don't try to get from someone else what must come from within you.* Your hunt for a partner may be encumbered by inner obstacles and unresolved baggage ---- insecurities, not knowing who you are, few skills to communicate openly, a discomfort with intimacy. You may have trouble balancing on the elusive edge of healthy vulnerability. Emotional closeness with someone may push your dependency buttons and make you feel like a helpless child, a scary state indeed.

As a result, you don't look for adult love that enhances your life. Instead you all too often search for the kind of unconditional love that you didn't get as a child and tolerate being treated badly. Or fearing real intimacy, you enter safe "nonrelationships" in which you never let anyone get close to you at all. (These issues were explored in Chapter 2.)

Marriage is a poor cure for feeling lost, scared, overwhelmed by life, or bored, or for having problems balancing your checkbook! A good relationship requires two self-sustaining adults, each capable of standing alone. An analogy: You may choose to let your partner drive on a trip, but since you are both good drivers, at any time, you can easily take over the wheel yourself.

• *One way or another, actively connect with someone else.* People rob banks because that's where the money is. Similarly, you must run an ad, answer an ad, list with an agency, ask friends to fix you up, or get out of the house and be where other potential partners are ---- unless the neighbor downstairs is fantastic or the mailperson is a charmer and up for grabs. You know that in order to get a job, you have to make a concerted effort, but you may fool yourself into believing that a perfect partner will magically appear.

Go to places or engage in activities that you genuinely enjoy. Even if you find no one special, you still can have a good time. If you go somewhere or do something you truly don't like, even if you do meet someone, you may end up having little in common with that person. (And of course if you don't meet anyone special or if you're not engaged in an activity of interest to you, the whole experience may feel like a waste of time.)

In an attempt to find the love of her life, a single woman friend of mine, politically quite liberal, first went to a Democrats' singles group. She found the conversation delightful, but a charming man who showed interest in her turned out to be married. With him she had a great present but no future. Several months later she went to a Republican singles group with a girlfriend. She told me that the food was far better than it had been at the Democrats' group, but the men she met were too conservative and could talk about little other than stocks and bonds.

In any gathering, incidentally, it doesn't matter whether a man or a woman makes the first move. What's said isn't that important either. But someone needs to risk the first move or word. On a visit to Florence, Italy, I saw a giant clock in one of the main plazas of the city. The presence of the clock didn't stop people from using the opening line, *"Che ora e?"* [What time is it?] with potential dates. I met my husband at a weekend retreat on occult psychology. Having recently studied Spanish and then learning he was of Latin heritage, I used the opening line, "Do you speak Spanish?" It wasn't particularly creative, but enough to start a conversation that eventually led to much more.

Chances to meet others occur everywhere. While sitting at the counter of a small restaurant, I happened to see a couple, probably in their early sixties, come in and sit across from me. Rather than say a word to each other, the woman immediately took out a book to read and the man became completely engrossed in his newspaper. They ordered their meals and ate but still shared nothing. I assumed that they were long married and had simply gotten in the habit of going through life in parallel tracks, communicating little. So I was surprised when a bit later the man got up and left by himself.

Only then did I realize they weren't together. More important, they had missed the possibility of connecting. Who knows, perhaps they were both in other relationships. Ponderer that I am, however, I saw the potential for a romance that never began.

• *If someone is interesting and responsive to you, move from small talk to setting up an opportunity to get better acquainted.* People become so carried away with the mystique of dating that they forget it's simply a method to decide with whom you would like to spend more time. Go for a walk; have a cup of coffee. If you were buying a house or a car, you would pay experts to check out your possible purchase. Not so with a prospective partner, for this decision is much too personal. So you must date ---- do your own legwork.

Pay attention to the place where the other person is in life: Satisfied or unhappy? Peaceful inside or dealing with too many unresolved issues? For example, does he need a constant stream of compliments in order to feel secure? Does she call up her girlfriend before making any decisions?

In the getting-to-know-someone-else stage, you need to develop proficiency in being able to trust another person, one step at a time. This process means disclosing yourself at a pace that correctly gauges the other person's ability and willingness to care and be there for you. Tune into your gut feelings. With practice, you can sense when an emotional connection feels safe: Is the other person kind, thoughtful about your needs and supportive of your interests? Do you feel pushed to tell or do things which make you uncomfortable? Are silences relaxed or uneasy? Do you feel a warm glow or a cool distance when you are together? Do you lose track of time or are you constantly checking your watch?

Communicate clearly what you need and what you want. No one can read your mind in spite of the illusion that "true love knows all." Since you are obviously imperfect, don't expect the other person to be flawless. But do be honest with yourself if the other person has traits that drive you up the wall. Incidentally, there's no need to tell about intimacies of past relationships. Save these for your friends from high school days, your Twelve-Step companions, or your therapist.

Choosing your life companion is a very personal endeavor. No one can do it for you. Over the years, I've introduced a number of friends, feeling that they'd be perfect for each other, but I've had no luck. The only exception was one memorable matchmaking triumph.

At the time of this tale, Natasha, Dutch and beautiful, had no partner. Though she is extremely self-sufficient, I was sorry to see our pet rabbit go through life alone, living on the back porch in her own little house with two Christmas trees from last year, loads of vegetables, and frequent visits from neighboring squirrels.

Since the porch is right outside my office, not only does our family enjoy Natasha's antics but so do my patients, some of whom are quite knowledgeable about rabbits. One day at the end of her session, a patient comments that a neutered male would be a perfect companion for solitary Natasha.

This comment gets me thinking about the possibilities. After talks with other "rabbit consultants," we learn that the perfect matchmaker, Judy, of the House Rabbit Society, is but a car ride away.

Several days later, directions and map in hand, Natasha in box, and thirteen-year-old Francesca beside me, we set forth eastward to meet Judy at a place where some ten or twelve rabbits await new homes. A few have already been paired off. Several are alone, one, a long-haired magnificent looking male Angora who needs daily combing, and Peter, a male Dutch, smaller than Natasha with black rather than grey coloring, but clearly a "good looker."

Judy brings Peter upstairs. We take Natasha out of her box and place both rabbits together in a small enclosed front room while we humans ---- Judy, her husband, Francesca, and I ---- sit, stand, gape, and talk. Judy points out some scars on poor Peter's back from a meeting the previous week when a first encounter with another potential partner had not gone well!

The two rabbits go back and forth between ignoring and approaching each other. Peter's the one who occasionally meanders over to Natasha's end of the room and attempts to mount her; Natasha responds by huffing and puffing and scampering away.

Francesca stares intently and silently at all their comings and goings. Meanwhile, I make lots of what I think are funny remarks about this first date: Is the chemistry right? Do they have enough in common? Is he too pushy? Is she too gun-shy? Judy has only a slight sense of humor, her nice German husband, none. But I continue to make wisecracks. Not only do I find the situation hilarious, but I'm covering my nervousness about whether I will be seen as fit mother-in-law for Peter by a pleasant young couple I've never met before and am unlikely ever to meet again.

We humans continue to talk for some twenty minutes while Peter and Natasha alternately chase and ignore each other. Because they have not actively fought, the consensus is that Natasha and Peter have an excellent chance of living happily ever after. And apparently I have passed the "good-enough parent-in-law" test.

Days, weeks, months later, they continue to nuzzle regularly. Life doesn't get better than this.

• *Let go of people who aren't right for you ---- those with too many problems; those with whom you don't share enough common values; those with whom you have no magical chemistry. If you* have been well-launched during your growing-up years, you still have to search a lot to find someone with whom you experience mutual attraction and share enough values and interests. The task is even harder if you have not observed models of happiness in your family of origin ---- if your parents stayed together but fought openly or simmered silently, or if they fell apart and neither one went on to a satisfactory relationship. For you then have no example of the give-and-take in healthy relationships cemented together by mutual love, respect, and appropriate interdependence.

As a friend of mine said while struggling to make his own marriage viable, "The family I came from was no help. My alcoholic father made a lot of money, and my mother was a martyr and stuck with him."

A healthy relationship should be able to survive what I call the "Desert Island Test." If the two of you are stranded on a desert island with no one else around, you have enough love, lust, care, and concerns to keep life interesting and fun. The wedding is just the beginning. (In fact, I have a theory that the more elaborate the wedding, the shorter the marriage ---- though feel free to prove me wrong. Pick your mate carefully!)

Don't stay with someone who constantly criticizes you and/or tries to make you over ---- someone who pressures you to eat differently, lose weight, drink less, change your wardrobe or hairstyle, be more orderly, rearrange your furniture, avoid certain relatives or friends, play a sport or attend an event you dislike, or change other personal habits. Similarly, don't you try to make the other person over or orchestrate his or her life. If the two of you ---- unedited ---- don't fit each other's tastes, don't stay miserably glued together 'til death do you part. (And horrors be, you might even get stuck together in an afterlife!)

As tempting as it is to hang on to a not-good-enough relationship just because it appears to be better than nothing ---- "Hey, we already know each other's histories and pet peeves" ---- don't do it. Loving someone with too many problems can turn you into a caretaker. The essence of a country western song, sung by a forlorn man, blared out at me from the car radio one day:

"Someday I'll get my life set straight."
She said, "Too bad it's too damn late.
Do what you can but I can't wait."

Too many people stay in not-good-enough relationships and turn them into not-good-enough marriages ---- marriages in which each party remains angry at the other for feeling caught and robbed of being happier; marriages filled with loneliness and/or infidelity; marriages covered over by pretense and denial.

Love becomes pain when two people share romantic love but not enough interests, much like Robert Redford's and Barbra Streisand's characters in *The Way We Were*. If two people share interests without enough romantic love, one of them might experience a dilemma similar to Ingrid Bergman's character in *Casablanca* ---- she's married to a "good" man but in love with another, Humphrey Bogart's character. And, as Francine Klagsbrun so aptly stated in *Married People, Staying Together in the Age of Divorce*, "Sex isn't everything, but it's an awful lot." None of these bases for a relationship are optimum. All in their own way are tragedies.

If you're reluctant to make a commitment to a particular person, try to determine the reasons for your hesitancy:

- Because of your age or stage of life, is it the wrong time for you to become settled?
- Does the other person have too many problems which affect you? For example, being a workaholic or jogaholic and never having time to be with you; still being

too tied up with parents or an ex-partner; always needing to be in control; not having any interests of his or her own; wanting to be waited on hand and foot; having temper tantrums about not getting his or her way; being miserable and not doing anything about it.

• Does the fit between the two of you not work well enough because of differences in personality or temperament?

• Are there obstacles within you, perhaps with roots in your past, which make a commitment feel overly scary or constraining? You can explore these issues in therapy, if you so choose.

Whatever the cause, if you don't feel ready to say "I do" out of your own desire, do not do so to please a partner or to avoid losing someone who is ready for a commitment. As the years go on, you don't want to look back and wish you had just said, "No."

After a friend of mine and his fiancée ---- both very much in love ---- decided that their relationship wasn't right for a lifetime, he came over to see me and broke down in tears. I asked if he thought that for him the breakup might hurt less than for someone who ran to alcohol, food, or another escape. "No," he answered. "I think that since I'm not insulated by anything, it hurts more. But I know I'll get beyond the pain, so I'm not scared."

When you truly belong to yourself, if a relationship doesn't work out, as painful as a breakup can be, you will survive it. Don't underestimate this certainty. You are no longer a helpless, dependent child without options or resources, even though the end of a relationship may temporarily feel that way. Cut your losses, laugh with friends about your foibles, regroup, and get on with your search.

• *Once you decide to stay with someone, give **first** priority to this relationship.* In a good relationship, you are there for each other through "thick" and sometimes a lot of "thin." When you put out your hand, you know that your partner will immediately take it; when you need support, he or she stands by. You don't play games or keep score. If either of you is involved in a particular project, at work or at home, without resentment you assist each other ---- whether it is a business trip, a presentation, an art show, a job interview, or a fancy dinner. And the longer you live together, the more unthinkable it is to even imagine life without each other.

Although happy married life should bring infinite romance and joy, it is also filled with unromantic day-to-day tasks like grocery shopping, cleaning up the house, paying bills, and so on and so on and so on. Even when you are occupied with the mundane, however, doing it with and for your loved one feels far better than doing it only for yourself. When you disagree, which any two independent people will do, decide which issues are worth seeing through to a compromise and which are best to let go and forget. You can drop arguments about where to park the car, who left a mess in the living room, and who didn't replace the empty roll of toilet paper within minutes.

Most important, accepting each other as you are is a bit like ordering the "Blue Plate Special" in a restaurant. If the "Blue Plate Special" is baked chicken, mashed potatoes, and cooked carrots, you can't substitute fried potatoes for the mashed ones or broccoli for the carrots. The meal comes as a package deal, and so does your partner. Happy marriages rest on a lot of love and good will; a balance between togetherness and separateness ---- in which you respect each other's right to space and privacy; a certain amount of upkeep from each other; a minimum of nagging; and a readily available sense of humor. You also need daily courtesies and an absence of "pot shots" at each other's lives ---- activities, friends, relatives.

As a result of your efforts, if you have the courage to create an exciting, original script with someone, it won't be an answer to life, but it can certainly be a grand adventure in life!

So ask yourself a few key questions:

• "Do I want a *permanent* traveling companion in life?" There is nothing wrong with going it on your own or only letting others be close to you on a temporary basis.

• "Am I willing to put energy into looking for someone and willing to let go of unhealthy or not-good-enough relationships?"

• "Once I find someone, is it worth it to me to give top priority to maintaining and enjoying the relationship?"

And as Piglet said to Pooh Bear when Pooh was having a long conversation with himself filled with questions, "And what did you answer yourself?"

Finding and staying with the "right one" may sound like an impossible task, but here's the good news: You only need one companion. So if you persist with realistic expectations, there is no reason for your search to be in vain.

FOURTEEN

Parenthood Brings Joy, Humility, And Grey Hair

Having a baby is something like
having your house leveled by a tornado
and winning the lottery, both on the same day.
                    ---- Barbara Kingsolver

E ndless musing about the errors of my parents and grandparents ---- and everyone else's parents ---- has convinced me. I can and must be the "perfect parent." This impossible goal can become absurd at times, especially when I think one of my children might unnecessarily miss out on a happy experience. Judge for yourself...

Mario, twelve, was to play in a soccer game on a Thursday afternoon. He usually takes his sports equipment to school and later gets a ride to the soccer field. On this particular day, however, the predicted rain has already started. Mom's advice: "Don't bother taking your soccer gear."

As the day wears on, the drizzle stops, the clouds lift and the sun comes out. Poor Mario. Obviously the soccer game will go on as planned, but he will be unable to play because I told him to leave his soccer equipment at home. What kind of mother am I?

But there's hope! A one-hour break between patients gives me just enough time to grab Mario's gear, dash over to his school, and find him in science class, surprised and embarrassed when Mom delivers the large plastic sack. As I rush out of the building, I bump into a young student, who, mistaking me for a teacher, asks for directions to one of the offices. "Sorry, I can't help," I answer. "I'm only a busy mother, frantically bringing something to my son." He reassures me, "Don't worry, you gave birth. That's enough."

Little does he know!

* * *

Because I started this book with "pot shots" at the difficulties of surviving our own childhoods and our parents' idiosyncrasies, it's only fitting to come full circle and discuss being a parent myself. Not that everyone must fill life with this particular venture. For those who do, though, a new dimension of living unfolds. And those who don't will undoubtedly leave a mark on the next generation in other ways ---- as an aunt or uncle, teacher, therapist, coach, or neighbor. However you may touch them ---- and they you ---- children not only add a rich dimension to your own life, but give you a chance to try your hand at launching a next generation of productive citizens into the world.

The Demands of Parenthood

Parenting is far more demanding than you imagined it would be. Taking a small bundle without operating instructions home from the hospital should have warned you of the uncertainty of what was to come. Probably, though, since you were so ecstatic, you thought the process would be a piece of cake once you got the swing of it ---- seeing the foibles of friends and relatives with their children would make you an instant expert.

In no way did you or could you anticipate how children affect your life. Once born, they would be far more important to you ---- far more dear ---- than you could have ever foreseen.

There are periods when you can give yourself respite and pat yourself on the back. The majority of the time, however, raising children is a mind-boggling undertaking. Once you have children, it's not all right to cop out on your responsible new role. The buck stops with you. Someone else's welfare is now at stake. Whether or not you got solid "roots" and "wings" from your own parents, it's up to you to try to give them to your children.

Establishing *roots* means physically and emotionally grounding your children ---- being there for them ---- often when you are so drained you can barely be there for yourself ---- trying to give hugs, read stories, listen to their concerns, shoot "hoops", help with homework that's left until the last minute.

Bestowing *wings* means granting independence in the "right" amounts at the "right" times, to fit *your children's* readiness and needs and *not* yours ---- trying to let them choose clothes, walk to school by themselves, drive their friends to the movies in the family car. Not that "letting go" is easy. Sometimes it's a Herculean task, fraught with pain, anguish, and tears. But the reward comes when you know the joy of raising independent, well-adjusted, happy kids!

Long ago I saw a cartoon picturing an exhausted mother nursing her baby and lamenting, "I don't know if this is the end of the last feeding or the beginning of the next." There are no relief shifts, no weekend or holiday vacations, and no time off for good behavior.

Establishing "Roots"

Giving children security and space to grow in ways appropriate to their needs is an awesome task. The unconditional love you feel for your growing child is only the beginning, but the essential beginning. For unless a child is truly loved, nothing else can make up for it.

Although loving a small baby may seem simple, often it is not. A baby may come into the world at a time when you yourself are going through a difficult emotional or financial period, or your marriage is in crisis. And though I never used to believe it, I'm now convinced that all babies are not equally lovable. Some are naturally easy to love, but others, because of their temperaments, may be superindependent and push you away. Ideally, as parents, you are able to respond to the unique style of each individual child, but this process can be trying. Bonding with a particular child may require lots of persistence and patience, sometimes in the midst of blatant rejection, a feeling that can dig into pockets of pain leftover from your own childhood.

As children get bigger, so do the challenges. Reasoning with young children can be a no-win, frustrating situation, as any seasoned parent knows. I once overheard a wonderful bathroom conversation between a mother and her three-year-old son:

"Wash your hands," she said.

"They're not dirty," he answered.

"Wash them anyway."

"I don't need to."

"You just went to the toilet."

"I didn't touch it."

"You flushed."

"My hands are clean."

"There are germs."

"I don't see anything."

At this point the woman threw up her hands and sternly said:

"Wash your hands!"

It's especially hard to parent when growing children don't "child" the way they are supposed to. They don't eat or sleep when you feel they should, their needs keep disrupting yours, and their weird judgement can scare the devil out of you. I still vividly remember four-year-old Francesca walking alone the five blocks from nursery school to our house, crossing busy streets ---- only one with a stoplight ---- so that we wouldn't have to bother picking her up on a day that school got out early. She was proud. We were wrecks.

Day-to-day experiences with children can range from cute to scary as youngsters play out adult scenes through children's eyes. A loving partner, friend, or therapist can be of great help and support during rough (or smooth) times.

Social values change and parents' leanings vary, but children's basic needs ---- in addition to the essential, unconditional love ---- don't change. Children need adult figures who are constant and available to help them feel good about themselves; to model themselves after; to learn to trust others; to leave them on their own gradually ---- when they're developmentally ready at each new stage of growth. (Independence granted too soon may feel like abandonment.)

Part of being a constant and available parent is spending quantity as well as quality time with your children ---- it's in your best interest and your children's. Juggling schedules can be complex. Don't squeeze in important interactions when you're drained from work or other commitments outside the family and your children are tired from school and their own activities. Instead, try to set aside specific periods of time each day just to be there with and for them. With honest soul-searching, you'll find a healthy balance between being a parent and "having a life."

Sometimes you can't be with your children as much as you'd like, especially if money is short or your career needs beckon. There will also be times you'll feel tempted to put work or the attainment of material goods unnecessarily ahead of your children's needs. Keep your priorities straight. This applies to fathers as well as mothers. Your children belong at the top of the list.

When you must be away from your children, good child care is essential. Your children need positive experiences with constant, dependable caregivers. The hidden costs of inadequate child care can be tragic: You may know from your own childhood, if you had to fend for yourself prematurely, you were left feeling lost inside. Because of this, as an adult, rather than being free to deal with complex challenges, you frantically search for the security and nurturance you never received in childhood. Select caretakers cautiously, especially if you are gone long hours.

Though it may seem forever that children are little and need you, they grow up fast and move on into their own lives. Being around your children as they grow up enables you to share in important milestones —— not only a baby's first steps and first words, but older children's "right on" observations: Mario, then age four, said to me, "Mommy, when I grow up, you'll have to feed ducks by yourself." Don't have regrets. The time with them doesn't come back. You've got to be there or you miss it.

Children will test your value system; holding steady demands strength. Your children may label you mean or old-fashioned if you don't let them go to undersupervised parties or stay out late in unsavory neighborhoods. They may envy latchkey peers with seemingly free reign and want that freedom for themselves. And how difficult it is to ride with the flow of your children's choices ---- clothes, hairdos, activities, politics, lifestyles, friends ---- perhaps significantly different from what you'd choose for them. You must bite your tongue rather than make unwelcome, "clever" sarcastic remarks. Not easy.

Oh, children can be masterful at guilt-producing words and sorrowful looks that attempt to pierce the heart of any parent who doesn't go the extra nine-thousand yards ---- "But Mom, *everyone else's* parents do that." Strong parents must remain firm against such tactics, lest they end up forgoing all adult-only outings, living in their cars as "go-fers" and chauffeurs, letting their children stay up every night to watch late television, giving extravagant allowances, and/or regularly preparing made-to-order specialty meals. To be "constant and available" for your children doesn't mean you should be their servant.

And how do you prepare your children to become productive citizens of society? A sensitive woman I know answered by asking two thought-provoking questions: "What does the world owe them?" and "What are you teaching your children that they owe the world?" You must help them gain the skills they'll need so that they can contribute to the solutions ---- not the problems ---- in society.

Guiding your children ---- giving them roots ---- is indeed an art. Too little direction and they fend for themselves by making choices without understanding the consequences ---- like dropping out of school, not realizing how this decision will affect their adult lives. But too much guidance and you risk suffocating them in your "good advice." Then they may rebel by being irresponsible, which can lead to self-destructive and dangerous results. Finding that balance between too little and too much guidance is not easy.

Bestowing "Wings"

Worrying is a dirty job, but somebody has to do it. The art of gradually stepping out of the "worrying role" in your children's lives and handing the reins over to them ---- bestowing wings ---- is a learned skill and I am still learning. As my friends and relatives know, I consistently work overtime in the worry department when it comes to my children. Sometimes it becomes ridiculous, particularly in hindsight.

One summer before starting middle school where he would know few of the other children, Mario was playing shortstop on a San Francisco tournament baseball team. Since the transition to a new school is never easy, I was glad his abilities in baseball would enable him to play on his school team, a source of new friends.

When I found out from another baseball mother that sixth-grade boys were not allowed to play on the school team, however, I spent the next couple of months worrying about how to break the bad news to Mario. A week before school started, I finally shared the sad reality with him. He matter-of-factly responded, "Oh, I heard that from the other kids at the beginning of the summer." And all my worrying for naught!

Parents don't have to look far to find more to worry about: How much, and at what age, do you shield your children from the unfairness and disappointments of life? When do you allow them to face these realities? Will your children be treated fairly by teachers? Will relationships to their friends work out? Will they be accepted in new situations? Will enough players show up so that the baseball team won't have to forfeit? We want the best for our children, and some of us will stop at nothing to direct and protect them. So we worry.

One world-class worrier outdid me, though. She called on my Saturday evening radio show to say she was very concerned about how her son was spending his money. As she went on, I discovered that she was eighty-eight ---- and worried about how her son was spending his retirement fund.

Once a parent, always a parent!

To stay on course, it helps to have tremendous mental fortitude, the support of a network of friends and relatives, the late-night thinking of a good companion, the realization that you are older than your children, and the insight to know that getting drunk is no solution. You operate on "a wing and a prayer" and often little else, groping in the dark to do the "right thing," whatever that is.

Watching Them Fly

Then there is adolescence, perhaps the most difficult time for parents to remember that they really want to give their children "wings." As my own children went through adolescence, I found myself eating most of the brilliant words of advice I'd given my patients and friends in the past. When you're not the parent of a particular teenager, you see a restless, struggling young person as interesting and to be admired. If you are the parent of such a teenager, however, your perspective changes completely. You're faced with someone who seems never to have heard your fantastic words of wisdom and who appears to make irrational and sometimes very poor decisions.

This situation may be made far worse if the rebellious teenager rides on the shoulders of an adult who can't or won't set limits. These shoulders may be yours or those of a well-meaning but meddling relative, teacher, coach, or neighbor. The result can be horrendous as the teenager acts out someone else's problems or becomes caught in a conflict between adults.

Even under the best of circumstances, however, launching a teenager is a rough job. During one stressful period when Andrea was communicating little and I was worrying a lot, on most days I looked like "death warmed over." One night I happened to be driving a twentyish young woman home from a meeting. When she saw I was upset and asked what was wrong, I muttered some general comment about my concerns about Andrea. My companion responded to my disheveled appearance and my frustrations: "My God, I had no idea what my mother was going through!" We don't get grey hair from nothing! (Incidentally, several years later Andrea told me how much it meant to her that her father and I continued to ask her to join the family even when she always answered, "No.")

I remember swapping teenager stories with the librarian at one of our children's schools, herself the mother of six grown children. She immediately understood everything I said, and with the clarity that comes from first-hand experience, she stated the guidelines that got her family through this period: "Keep the door open and don't ask too many questions." That about sums it up.

The only suggestion I have for surviving our adolescents' adolescence is that we all exchange teenagers with our friends. Then each parent would raise someone else's child and remain cool, objective and wise during critical junctures. And each teenager would think that the advice given was brilliant and helpful.

If you find you're recycling too much pain from your own childhood onto your children, get professional help. The cycle of neglect and/or abuse can be broken. Your history does not have to seal your children's fates.

Remember that your children are not reincarnations of you. If you have done the parenting job well, you've helped them become themselves, nurturing their strengths so that they can follow their own dreams. You have not pushed them to have your likes and dislikes or to live life for you.

As my children graduate from each level of school, I'm reminded how short our time is together in the parent-child relationship. How important and essential it is to let them go into their own orbits so we can have happy adult-to-adult relationships, and they can become independent, self-confident adults. Staying on the sidelines when they choose partners is of course the ultimate test. The best you can do is to accept and love whomever they love and, as a friend of mine said, "Fill the house with flowers for their weddings."

The Ultimate Joys of Parenthood

Fortunately the reward for the hard work of being a parent is the joy of seeing your children become nice human beings, who continue to be part of your life, and memories of many precious moments long after the anxiety and anger are forgotten...

Many years ago, our family was finally returning to our much beloved California from a too-long detour in Cleveland, Ohio. Packing at a furious pace, we stacked boxes everywhere and time seemed short. Suddenly, Andrea, then age five, said, "Let's bake cookies." That's crazy, I thought. All the cooking utensils and cookie tins have been packed, and more important, we didn't have time. But a beam of light in my head said, "Stop and bake cookies." And that is exactly what we did. In the midst of the chaos, we had a wonderful time and paid attention to what is important in life...

Late one night Andrea knocked on our door, complaining that three-year-old Michelle was keeping her awake with a song. We thought Andrea was exaggerating and urged her to go back to sleep. When she knocked again we finally came out to hear Michelle singing at the top of her lungs, "Oh do you know the Muffin Man, the Muffin Man,"...

At one family Christmas gathering, Mamacita, my mother-in-law, had prepared an elegant nativity scene. All of us gathered around to admire it and then became busy with the preparation of dinner. A bit later glancing at the nativity scene, I was surprised to find the baby Jesus missing. We then saw two-year-old Francesca sitting on the couch with her sweater around baby Jesus, gently rocking him to sleep...

Three-year-old Mario looked for his socks at nursery school, getting ready to go home. Most of the children's socks were of the standard white cotton variety. After someone pointed out to Mario that he was mistakenly putting on Benji's socks, he suddenly yelled, "I hate Benji!" "Why?" I ask. "Because he put his name on my socks," answered my frustrated young son...

As your children get older, they may give gifts of themselves back to you. They offer you helpful rides in their cars and casually mention, "It's nothing compared to all the rides you gave me when I was growing up." The phone rings as you return from vacation, "just to check if you are okay." (You also found a delicious pasta salad in the refrigerator and the house clean.) They describe in detail subjects you know little about, as eager to share information with you as you are to learn more about their views of the world. They're supportive and patient as they tutor you in sports and other activities in which their skills now surpass yours.

In spite of parental blunders and paranoia, by and large, children mature. And so do parents: "It is not the parent who raises the child but rather, the child who raises the parent." How true. Parenthood provides you with a second chance to grow up.

And just as you can forgive your parents' errors, your children forgive you the same. If you honestly try to launch them well, not only will they forgive you for not doing it perfectly, but equally important, you can forgive yourself.

FIFTEEN

Today Is All We Have —
Basta Cosi

To enjoy life, take big bites.
Moderation is for monks.
----Anonymous

T he art of living well is to weave through the memories of the past and the hurdles of the present and still find joy in today.

*   *   *

The line is long, but I decide to wait. There is no hurry. I need to pick up the food for the day ---- cheese, meat, bread, olives and wine. Our family will have some kind of adventure, and we always feel freer when we carry our own supplies.

My mind drifts off. The morning has started out as have all the mornings since we have been in Rome. Early each day, before sunlight fills the sky completely, we are awakened by the vendors in the nearby outdoor market. They bustle around, finding their places and setting out fruit, vegetables and other wares. Soon after, the loud noises of the metal protectors being raised in front of each store are heard. Then, like on a stage, people meandering here and there gradually fill the streets as the day goes into full gear.

Already I have picked up the vegetables and fruit and exchanged small talk with the vendor. As has been true each morning we meet, she and I speak of our children, three of ours still with us, hers already off on their own.

Today is different because it is our last day in Rome. We will leave this evening to return to the United States, and I need to say good-bye. I brought the vegetable vendor pictures of San Francisco, a John F. Kennedy silver coin, and several other small mementos as farewell remembrances. She did not let me pay for the carrots. We hugged and I cried. My family and I have only been in Rome for twenty days, but this woman has become very much part of our lives here. Though she has worked in this market for thirty years and our family tries to visit every few years, it is unlikely I will ever see her again. And even if I do, it will be in a different chapter of my life. I feel sad not because I have known her well or deeply or long. Rather, the parting is bittersweet because our relationship has been so simple, and saying goodbye to her has brought up all the good-byes I have ever said in my life.

Whenever I go to Rome ---- as often as money and time allow ---- within the first few days I go to visit my brother's grave. He is buried on a pretty little hill beneath a lovely tree in the protestant cemetery, the "Cimiterio Acatolico per Stranieri." It is a peaceful place. My brother is in good company. Not far away rest Keats and Shelley and many others who wandered to Rome to try to find something that they couldn't find in their own countries, or in themselves.

Each time I visit the cemetery and first catch sight of my brother's tombstone, temporarily I am demolished by tears. Each time I want to scream at the top of my lungs, "No ---- it's not true ---- it's not fair!" Although I have lived most of my adult life without my brother, I especially miss him when I have a good story to share. He would have enjoyed hearing how his little sister ended up on the radio. He would have been furious at the con artist who took my friend George. He would have laughed with me at the matchmaking for our rabbits, Natasha and Peter. He would have loved to hear the sagas of our children. I am outraged at his not being here and my never being able to see him again.

Rome, eternal city, as much as I love you, I also hate you. Not only were you unable to save my brother but in addition, you go on as if nothing ever happened, just as you have for centuries and centuries. You lend bits and pieces of yourself to all who pass through, yet smugly you know that you belong to yourself and will survive while those of us who temporarily savor your charm will come and go and before long, be gone.

The line has moved a little. I can now see all the cheese, and I am trying to decide how many etti [one hundred grams] and which kind to purchase. My mind goes back to the time I was living and working in Rome many years ago. I had taken off for a week of skiing at Cortina D'Impezzio in the north. I met some people while on vacation, and on the way back we wandered around the town too long and almost missed the tram. As I rushed and barely caught it, I fell back into my American neurotic mentality. Sensing my anxiety, the kind elderly conductor asked me why I was in such a hurry. In my make-do Italian, I answered, "I need to catch this tram, or I will miss the train for Rome." He smiled and calmly said, "You are young and life is long. If you don't catch the train today, you will catch one tomorrow. You mustn't worry about such things."

The line still moves slowly. I look at the faces around me. Clearly the people have little material wealth, but they don't look unhappy. Are they wiser about living life as it is ---- that days start with *buon giornos;* that they are filled by the necessities of life mixed with pleasant interactions with others; that days ultimately end with the exchange of *bona nottes?* Formalities, brief interactions and moments of connection with others ---- perhaps that is all there is.

I glance over at the owner of the store. What is his life like? He looks sixty or so years old. He works seven days a week ---- up at four in the morning to help with the baking, maybe even works from noon to four while the store is closed, and is still there late at night. Is this his only life? Does he have a wife, a family? He's gentle toward people and yet intrudes into their lives, too. I know this because one day when I was practicing my rusty Italian on him, he started to grill me at an inappropriately personal level. There is much unspoken in him. Is it anger, resignation, desperation, loneliness? Are his work, store, customers, and neighbors his whole existence? Is there peace within him or just a letting go of any dreams and an acceptance of each day as the totality of life? Should I envy or pity him? Has he ever lived beyond this block? Is he curious about other parts of the city, the country, the world?

It is almost my turn at the counter. I decide to get *un'etto* of prosciutto, *due etti* of my favorite smoked cheese, *un'etto* of olives, some fresh-smelling *pannini* [bread], and a good bottle of local wine. The man at the counter asks me, *"Basta cosi* [enough as is]?" I answer, *"Basta cosi."* And as I pay for my purchases and carry them out of the store, I know that I have everything I need. My husband and children are waiting for me. Yes, *basta cosi.* It is enough.

SIXTEEN

Everything Matters —
Nothing Matters

No matter what you do or don't do in your lifetime,
the size of your funeral will depend on the weather.
—— Anonymous

"Does it matter if I get some Bs or Cs?" asks Mario, who usually likes to get As. It's two days before graduation from middle school, and we're having one of those rare late-night mother-son talks when important issues are raised and no one holds anything back. "No," I say. "All that matters is that you keep doors open for what you may want in the future in school and career and life. Only you will know when it is important to work at your full capacity. You'd be exhausted if you did it all the time —— like making a gourmet dinner every single night. No one has that sort of time or energy.

"But sometimes, like in the Olympics, go all out, hit your stride, and do your personal best. You choose the arenas for your achievements —— art, writing, music, sports, math. It could be a speech, a presentation, a painting, or any other project. Every once in a while, just for you, let a challenge matter a great deal. Reach for your own goal and know that you can do no better. And regardless of the consequences or reactions from others, you can sit back and feel proud and peaceful, knowing that you have given your maximum effort, and your accomplishment is as complete as you can make it."

As we hug before he goes to bed, I realize that although I can give him my version of what matters, he'll have to discover his version for himself.

One of the many arts of life is caring deeply about some things, allowing them to matter a great deal, and at the same time being able to let them go and get on with other ventures. You must be at one with the process and yet not let the outcome make or break you —— whether you succeed or fail, win or lose, get the award or promotion or not.

From time to time I err and become too carried away with a project or cause and forget the clear thinking of the Reinhold Niebuhr prayer, "God grant me the serenity to accept the things I cannot change, the strength to change the things I can, and the wisdom to know the difference." I'm frightened and saddened, however, when people go to the other extreme and retreat from the action. They get caught in the acceptance part of the prayer and not only too readily accept the unacceptable, but don't try to change what rightfully can be changed. Or they become consumed by anger and bitterness and disengage themselves from letting anything matter at all.

Wayne, a sixty-one-year-old man, whom I know only casually, has followed many directions —— first law, then politics and now art. Divorced, he has grown children who live far away. Lately, he has been immersed in church issues. In the course of a recent conversation at a party, he mentioned that three close friends had died within the past ten months, one from a long and painful illness. When I expressed sympathy, he brushed my words aside with a quick response: "Undoubtedly it falls into an ultimate plan. We all must die sometime. There's no need for sadness." He then moved the conversation to pleasant impersonal topics, but I refused to let go.

I mentioned the tragic conditions in which so many people find themselves in the world ---- whether homelessness, hunger, poverty in general, or brutal, dictatorial regimes. But Wayne was unshakable. "Everything has a purpose," he said. "In some way it is all going as it was meant to." He looked detached and peaceful. I felt sick. Shortly afterward, Wayne excused himself and cheerfully went off to corner a new listener at the other end of the room.

During high school, I shared many after-school and weekend hours with Abby. We often talked into the wee hours of the morning, analyzing life, love, and the pursuit of happiness. She was feisty, loved challenges, and lived each day with zest.

After graduation, our paths led us in different directions ---- mine to college and medical school, Abby's to an early marriage and three children. She became heavily involved with community issues affecting her family and political issues close to her heart. Although at first we kept in touch with letters, occasional phone calls, and visits whenever I was back in town, after a few years we lost contact. Following a lapse of ten years, I again looked Abby up. She had become a bitter, angry stranger, resembling little the full-of-life friend I once knew. She told me that all the energy she had formerly spent to change the world was just "a ridiculous waste of time. You can't really make a difference. We were only fooling ourselves to think that it mattered."

In contrast, Mary, an eighty-year-old woman who had been married to my college counselor, stays vitally involved in life. Though widowed a number of years and scarred by more than her share of losses, she is back in the mainstream.

She's always occupied with her own creative ventures, yet finds time to visit her children and their families regularly. Fortunately for me, she also keeps in touch with friends. When I'm with Mary, she's extremely interested in my activities, and in addition, full of enthusiasm about her own. She helps in her community and stays politically active, continuing to fight for causes that matter to her, whether marching in rallies, giving time to help stuff envelopes, or writing to members of Congress. Mary is still passionate about everything and undoubtedly will be until the day she dies.

An anecdote told of two men who were walking close to the ocean's edge on sand strewn with beached starfish. The younger man kept leaning down to pick up starfish and throw them back into the water. The older one exclaimed, "There are too many to save. What difference does it make?" The younger man replied, "It makes a difference to the ones that get thrown back."

We have a choice: Stay with life or park by the wayside and be spectators. In spite of the overwhelming odds against righting most of life's wrongs, doing nothing is not a viable option! Dante (1265-1321) said, "The hottest places in Hell are reserved for those who, in time of great moral crisis, maintain their neutrality."

An item on the late evening news was the story about a twelve-year-old boy who had called the "911" hot line to report that his 49ers jacket had just been stolen. Though not hurt, he spoke through tears: "I spent all my money from my paper route to buy it." In the ensuing days, the police did not find the mugger but were so moved by the boy's story, they decided to take up a collection to buy the boy another jacket and present it to him at his middle school. When he was called out of class on the day of the presentation, awaited by his father and several policemen in the principal's office, he could only assume he was in trouble. Not so! As he proudly put on the new jacket and placed his hands in the pockets to check the fit, he discovered a $100 bill in each one.

Bad guys still get away with robbery and murder. On that particular day, however, some good guys made a difference to one young man, and to any of us who chanced to hear the heartwarming story.

My zeal occasionally gets me into ridiculous predicaments. When some parents of the opposing little league baseball team heckled our fourteen-year-old pitcher, I was incensed, especially since our team went on to lose by one run. It's bad enough when children tease another child. But when adults tease a child, I think it's a mortal sin.

So after the game, seeing a group of parents approaching from the other side, I immediately walked over to them and in no uncertain terms, told them what I thought about teasing the pitcher. I took their surprise to be a cover-up of their crime. I became angrier. As I went on lecturing, however, I realized I was delivering my irate sermon to the innocent ---- the parents who had just arrived for the next game! The real culprits had already left. As my children reassure me, no one will ever fault me for not speaking my mind.

I went to a local high school to watch Francesca, my fifteen-year-old daughter, in her first gymnastics competition. Although she had participated in dance since kindergarten days, she had been in gymnastics for only six weeks and had no previous experience in competitive sports.

When I asked the woman next to me when the meet would start, she told me her life history, including stories of bad men and bad drugs and a litany of complaints about her children. She finally wound down into, "Well, none of it matters, anyway."

I still hadn't learned when the meet would start and was about to ask again when suddenly the hall became quiet. A young student strode to the middle of the gym floor and began to belt out a beautiful rendition of the "Star-Spangled Banner." I glanced across the room at Francesca, who smiled back at me. She looked beautiful. It mattered that I was there.

I stayed up to watch my friend Shirley interviewed on a middle-of-the-night television show. It was her first such venture. Aired in the pre-home-video days, either you caught the action as it was happening or you didn't —— there was no chance for a replay. Because Shirley appeared at the end of the hour (and the first part didn't interest me), I took a short snooze. At least I meant it to be short. More tired than I realized, I slept right through the whole show. I was extremely annoyed at myself.

When I saw Shirley the next day, she asked how the interview had gone. I told her what happened and apologized profusely. She said, "Don't worry. It wasn't that important. It doesn't matter." She was wrong. It mattered to me.

When it is all over, what you did or didn't do will matter little. Whether you remained curious about nature or felt bored; whether holidays continued to bring wonderment or became a chore; whether you liked your work or lived for Friday; whether your relationships enriched your days or were just "okay"; whether you kept your integrity or lost it along the way —— it will all be history. But while you're living your life, *everything* matters.

If your childhood wasn't happy, if you've never made peace with important family members, if you've had more than your share of bad luck and losses, it is sad and it does matter. But what matters even more is that you not let the pain of the past and the unfairness of life rob you of making the best of what can be now.

Remember:

- Each day is a blank canvas.

- When opportunity knocks, ready or not, open the door.
- Choose your support system carefully.
- A traveling companion can enhance your journey.
- Parenthood brings joy, humility, and grey hair.
- Today is all we have —— *basta cosi.*

Before it's too late, may you have many fine adventures and good times with those you love. May you help anyone who crosses your path, attempt to change the injustices in the world that can be changed, and scream out in indignation at what should but can't be changed. And even when life hurts a lot, may you stay vulnerable and involved.

Each morning, once the children are off to school, it's time for my rounds of the animals. In addition to seeing that there is food and water for the rabbits, the cats, and the guinea pigs, today I check on our newest acquisition, a baby bird found yesterday on the ground. As I'm about to enter the room to look in on it, I cross my fingers hoping it will be all right. When I turn on the light, the little bird is sitting up on its heating-pad home, alive and lively, mouth open expectantly, ready for a couple of droppers full of watered-down oatmeal.

Everything matters, nothing matters.

Epilogue —
"To Be Or Not To Be"

Life is too short to drink bad wine.
                    —— Bumper sticker

"Being" —— though basically simple —— has endless variety, limited only by your imagination and the number of days in your lifetime. "Not being" —— though packaged in deceptively different wrappings —— contains colorless contents and is riddled with wasted opportunities.

"Being" is alive, and life, a boundless creative adventure. "Not being" is dead and essentially, an unlived life.

Some keys to remember about "being":

- Your life belongs to you and no one else.
- There is no right or wrong way to live it.
- You alone are responsible for making it meaningful.

Before it's over and you've missed too much, you still have time. But you must stop believing that the circumstances of your childhood seal your fate; that changes are out of your power; or that it is up to others to make you happy.

Will you settle for a safe script ---- a predictable, sometimes boring life ---- always pleasing others and finding excuses for not following your own dreams? Or will you courageously choose an original script ---- *Your Life* ---- pursuing and playing your own role ---- with passion?

To go all out and risk entering uncharted territories ----writing your own script ---- can be scary. But the alternative is never to truly live at all ---- a guaranteed tragedy.

* * *

What was, was.

What is, is.

What can be is up to you.

For Further Reading

I'd like to mention a few books, full of wisdom, that are fantastic fair- and foul-weather friends:

Forbes, Kathryn. *Mama's Bank Account*. New York: Harcourt, Brace and World, Inc., 1943.

Gibran, Kahlil. *The Prophet*. New York: Alfred A. Knopf, 1972.

Gunther, John. *Death Be Not Proud: A Memoir*. New York: Harper & Row, 1949.

Kopp, Sheldon. *An End to Innocence*. New York: Bantam Books, 1978.

Kushner, Harold S. *When Bad Things Happen to Good People*. New York: Avon Books, 1983.

Lindbergh, Anne Morrow. *Gift from the Sea*. New York: Pantheon Books, 1975.

Peter, Lawrence J., and Raymond Hull. *The Peter Principle*. New York: Bantam Books, 1969.

Shawn, Wallace, and Andre Gregory. *My Dinner with Andre*. New York: Grove Press, 1981.

In addition, you may have been lucky enough to have had a parent or other relative who read books to you when you were little. Or, as an adult, you might have discovered some of the great ones for yourself or read to your children or someone else's. In case you missed them, however, let me here mention a few of my all-time favorites, books I've read again and again to my own children that continue to touch me and remind me of what counts in life. All of these authors have written other wonderful books as well.

Anderson, Hans Christian. *The Emperor's New Clothes*. New York: Houghton Mifflin, 1949.

Bemelmans, Ludwig. *Madeline*. New York: Simon & Schuster, 1939.

Dahl, Roald. *Charlie and The Chocolate Factory*. New York: Bantam Books, 1984.

De Brunhoff, Jean. *The Story of Babar the Little Elephant*. New York: Random House, 1984.

Juster, Norton. *The Phantom Tollbooth*. New York: Random House, 1961.

Milne, A. A. *Winnie-the-Pooh*. New York: E. P. Dutton, 1926.

Saint-Exupery, Antoine de. *The Little Prince*. New York: Harcourt Brace Jovanovich, 1943.

Sendak, Maurice. *Where the Wild Things Are*. New York: Harper & Row, 1984.

Williams, Margery. *The Velveteen Rabbit*. New York: Harcourt Brace Jovanovich, 1922.

Zolotow, Charlotte. *The Sky Was Blue*. New York: Harper and Row, 1963.

MORE BOOKS WITH *IMPACT*

We think you will find these Impact Publishers titles of interest:

DON'T BELIEVE IT FOR A MINUTE!
Forty Toxic Ideas that are Driving You Crazy
Arnold A. Lazarus, Ph.D.,
Clifford N. Lazarus, Ph.D., and Allen Fay, M.D.
Softcover $9.95   192pp
Two psychologists and a psychiatrist debunk forty
common misbeliefs that can lead to depression,
anxiety and guilt.

MASTER YOUR PANIC
And Take Back Your Life!
Denise F. Beckfield, Ph.D.
Softcover $12.95   288pp
Self-help guidance for overcoming past hurts,
dealing with the reality of present-day life, and
building a foundation for better tomorrows.

BEYOND THE POWER STRUGGLE
Dealing With Conflict in Love and Work
Susan M. Campbell, Ph.D.
Softcover: $8.95   256pp
Resolve trouble and build win-win relationships in
love and on the job.

THE ASSERTIVE WOMAN: A New Look
Stanlee Phelps, M.S.W., and Nancy Austin, M.B.A.
Softcover: $11.95   256pp
Updated edition of the bestselling assertiveness book
for women.

Impact 🕮 *Publishers*®
POST OFFICE BOX 1094
SAN LUIS OBISPO, CALIFORNIA 93406

Please see the following page for more books.